4⁵⁰

CRASH ACTION
WINNERS
1944
LARKHILL

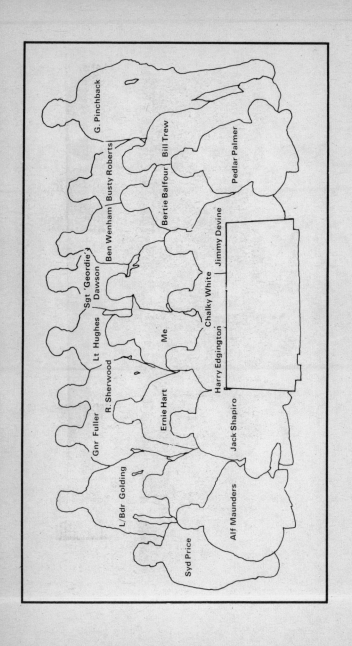

19 Battery on train to Embarkation Port – fighting off a ticket inspector

Penguin Books

'ROMMEL?'

'GUNNER WHO?'

Spike Milligan was born in Ahmednagar in India in 1918. He received his first education in a tent in the Hyderabad Sindh desert and graduated from there, through a series of Roman Catholic schools in India and England, to the Lewisham Polytechnic. Always something of a playboy, he then plunged into the world of Show Business, seduced by his first stage appearance, at the age of eight, in the nativity play of his Poona convent school. He began his career as a band musician but has since become famous as a humorous script writer and actor in both films and broadcasting. He was one of the main figures in and behind the infamous Goon Show. Among the films he has appeared in are: *Suspect, Invasion, Postman's Knock* and *Milligan at Large*.

Spike Milligan's published work includes *The Little Potboiler, Silly Verse for Kids, Dustbin of Milligan, A Book of Bits, The Bed-Sitting Room* (a play), *The Bald Twit Lion, A Book of Milliganimals, Small Dreams of a Scorpion, Transports of Delight, The Milligan Book of Records, Games, Cartoons and Commercials, Dip the Puppy, William McGonagall: The Truth at Last* (with Jack Hobbs), *The Spike Milligan Letters* and *More Spike Milligan Letters*, both edited by Norman Farnes, *Open Heart University, The Q Annual, Unspun Socks from a Chicken's Laundry, The 101 Best and Only Limericks of Spike Milligan, There's a Lot of It About, The Melting Pot, Further Transports of Delight, The Looney: An Irish Fantasy* and *The Lost Goon Shows*. His unique and incomparable six volumes of war memoirs are: *Adolf Hitler: My Part in His Downfall, 'Rommel,' 'Gunner Who?', Monty: His Part in My Victory, Mussolini: His Part in My Downfall, Where Have All the Bullers Gone?* and *Goodbye Soldier*.

SPIKE MILLIGAN

'Rommel?'

'Gunner Who?'

A Confrontation in the Desert

Edited by Jack Hobbs

PENGUIN BOOKS

PENGUIN BOOKS

Published by the Penguin Group
27 Wrights Lane, London w8 5tz England
Viking Penguin Inc., 40 West 23rd Street, New York, New York 10010, USA
Penguin Books Australia Ltd, Ringwood, Victoria, Australia
Penguin Books Canada Ltd, 2801 John Street, Markham, Ontario, Canada l3r 1b4
Penguin Books (NZ) Ltd, 182–190 Wairau Road, Auckland 10, New Zealand

Penguin Books Ltd, Registered Offices: Harmondsworth, Middlesex, England

First published by Michael Joseph 1974
Published in Penguin Books 1976
17 19 20 18

Made and printed in Great Britain by
Richard Clay Ltd, Bungay, Suffolk
Set in Monotype Baskerville

To my dear brother Desmond
who made my boyhood happy and with whom
I have never had a cross word,
mind you he drives his wife mad

Thanks

Once again I am deeply grateful to Mrs Chater Jack, widow of our C.O. and late Lt Colonel Chater Jack, M.C., D.S.O., for the use of the private letters, diaries and documents which she so willingly lent me and is patient enough to let remain in my possession for this second volume, also to Al Fildes for his diary, and Harry Edgington for permission to publish his letters, plus the lads from the Battery who lent me the odd photo or letter, to Mr Rose and Mr Greenslade of the Ministry of Defence – to Mr Mayne of the War Museum for the loan of photographs – and to Syd Price for photos he took during the War and to BART H. VANDERVEEN for permission to use two photographs of the Humber Snipe wireless truck and also thanks to Derek Hudson for the loan of the photograph of Anthony Goldsmith.

S.M.

19 Bty 56 Heavy embarking for Africa

Prologue

Of the events of war, I have not ventured to speak from any chance information, nor according to any notion of my own. I have described nothing but what I saw myself, or learned from others of whom I made the most careful and particular enquiry.

Thucydides. Peloponnesian War.

I've just jazzed mine up a little.

Milligan. World War II.

Overture

H.Q. Afrika Korps — Tunis. Jan. 1943
Smell of German Ersatz Eggs, Sausages and Marlene
Dietrich.
A 'phone rings. General Stupenagel salutes it, and
picks it up.

STUPENAGEL: Speilen!

GOERING: Do you know were von Rommel is? This is
Urgent.

STUPENAGEL: General von Urgent?

GOERING: Don't make wiz zer fuck-about! — vere is
Rommel?

STUPENAGEL: He is in zer shit-house.

GOERING: Vot is he doing in zere at zis time of zer
morning.

STUPENAGEL: He is doing zer schitz he was bombed
all night.

GOERING: Donner Blitzen!

STUPENAGEL: He's in zer shit-house too.

GOERING: Listen! Ve have had Bad News!

STUPENAGEL: Dat sounds like bad news!

GOERING: Our spy, Mrs Ethel Noss, in zer Algiers
NAAFI, says dat zer Pritishers have brung zer heavy
Artillery into Africa.

STUPENAGEL: Gott no!

GOERING: Gott yes! Zey are going to make shoot-
bang-fire mit 200 pound shells.

STUPENAGEL: Oh, Ger-fuck!

GOERING: Tell Rommel, zer Führer wants him to got mit zer Panzer and make vid zer Afrika Korps, Schnell!

Scene changes to a German latrine in a Wadi near Shatter-el-Arab

Enter STUPENAGEL

STUPENAGEL: Rommel, vich one are you in?

ROMMEL: Number Zeben.

STUPENAGEL: You must go to Tunis at once.

ROMMEL: Let me finish going here first.

STUPENAGEL: Zere is a crisis out zere.

ROMMEL: Zere is a crisis in here; no paper. *(screams, sound of scratching)*

STUPENAGEL: Vat is ger-wrong?

ROMMEL: Itchy Powder on zer seat!

STUPENAGEL: Ach zer Pritish Commandos have struck again.

Now read on:

Jan : Feb

X Camp. Cap Matifou. Algeria

If you read the first volume of this trilogy, you will know that in Jan. 1943 19 Battery 56th Heavy Rgt R.A. had arrived in the continent of Africa, which couldn't have cared less. We were in 'X Camp,' soldiers under fourteen couldn't get in without their parents. Calling it 'X' for security was beyond comprehension because there, in foot high letters, was the sign 'No 201 PoW Camp.' I could hear the Gestapo 'Mein Führer, ve have cracked zer Britisher Code! X, it means 201 PoW Camp! Soon we will know what PoW means.' The Camp, situated up a dusty track fifty yards from the main Algiers Road, was a rectangle covering five acres surrounded by a double barbed wire fence fifteen feet high. The view was beautiful, the light clear, brilliant, like Athens on a midsummer day. Stretching to our left was a gradual curve of the coast with a laticlave of yellow sand and finally, Algiers proper, barely visible in the distance. To the right, turning crescent-like was another beach that terminated in a dazzling white lighthouse on Cap Matifou. This was all described in the Regimental diary thus: '*Arrived at X Camp, Cap Matifou.*' Whatever happened to Poetry?

Algeria

The ground was like rocks. The nights were rent with gunners groaning, swearing, twisting, turning and revolving in their tents.

Temperatures fluctuated. You went to sleep on a warm evening, by dawn it dropped to freezing. We had to break our tents with hammers to get out. Dawn widdles caused frost bitten appendages, the screams! 'Help, I'm dying of indecent exposure!' We solved the problem. I stuffed my Gas cape

19

with paper and made a mattress. Gunner Forest wrapped old Daily Mirrors round his body, 'I always wanted to be in the News,' he said, and fainted. Others dug holes to accommodate hips and shoulders.

At night we wore every bit of clothing we had, then we rolled ourselves into four blankets. 'We look nine months gone,' said Edgington. 'Any advance on nine,' I cried.

We slept warmly, but had overlooked the need to commune with nature, it took frantic searching through layers of clothing to locate one's willy, some never did and had to sleep with a damp leg. Gunner Maunders solved the problem! He slid a four foot length of bicycle inner tube over his willy, secured it round his waist with string, he just had to stand and let go. Jealous, Gunner White sabotaged it. As Maunders slept, fiend White tied knots in the bottom of the tube.

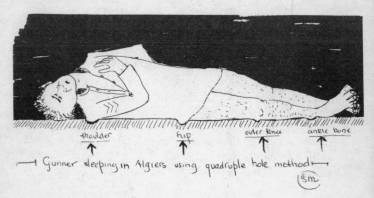

shoulder ↑   hip ↑   outer knee ↑   ankle bone ↑

⊢ Gunner sleeping in Algiers using quadruple hole method ⊢

(SM

Confined to Camp

It is night, Gunner Simpson is darning something which is four fifths hole and one fifth sock, 'I wonder when they'll let us into Algiers.' 'You gettin' randy then?' says Gunner White, 'because, we've all had our last shag for a long time.'

'Are there French birds in Algiers?'

'Yer. They're red 'ot. Cert Crumpet.'

'You shagged one then?'

Gunners Anti-Cold Sleeping Wear.

' No, but my dad told me abaht 'em in the first world woer.'

'They're not the same ones?'

One by one the soldiers would fall asleep. I lay awake, thinking, dreaming young man's dreams, jazz music would go through my head, I could see myself as Bunny Berrigan playing chorus after brilliant chorus in front of a big band surrounded by admiring dancers. Suddenly, without warning, 'Strainer' Jones lets off with a thunderous postern blast, he had us all out of the tent in ten seconds flat.

One freezing dawn we were awakened by a Lockheed Lightning repeatedly roaring over our camp. 'Go and ask that bastard if he's going by road,' says Edgington. I got outside just as the plane made another drive. I shouted 'Hope you crash you noisy bastard,' the plane raced seaward, hit the water and exploded. I was stunned. The gunners emptied from their tents to watch the flames burning on the sea. 'Poor Sod,' said a Gunner, and he was right. Reveille was sounding. 'Listen,' said Edgington cupping an ear, 'they're playing our tune.'

My day, by Gunner Milligan

Dear Diary, oh what a morning it's been.

0630.	*REVEILLE:*	*we were annoyed.*
0730.	*BREAKFAST:*	*Oh yum yum.*
0900.	*1ST PARADE:*	*Good morning darling!*
0915.	*DAILY TASK:*	*Who me?*
1300.	*LUNCH:*	*More boiled shit. Oh yum yum.*
1415.	*2ND PARADE:*	*Haven't we met before?*
1430.	*TASKS:*	*I've got back-ache Sarge.*
1645.	*FALL OUT:*	*Crash.*
1800.	*GUARDMOUNTING:*	*Quick. Under the bed!*

A word about the food. Crap. Hard biscuits, Soya Links, Bully Beef, jam, tea, every day, for *all* meals. The first weeks were spent route marching. The Army works like this. If a man dies when you hang him, keep hanging him until he gets used to it. Marches were made tolerable by Major

19 Battery Signallers attacking the Cook-house for second helpings at X Camp, Cap Matifou

Chater Jack* insisting we sing. A message would pass down the column 'Gunners Milligan, Edgington, White and Devine forward!' We'd gain the head of the column and to the tune of Vive la Compagnie, we'd sing:

SOLO: The might of the nation was wielded by one
OMNES: Vive la Joe Stalin!
SOLO: He isn't half knockin' the shit from the Hun!
OMNES: Vive la Joe Stalin . . . etc.

We were young, we were enjoying the new adventure, ninety-nine per cent of the lads had never been abroad, and this was a bonus in their lives even though it took a war to give it. Chalky White invented a new sound, on the first beat of the march you crashed your foot down, for the next three beats you trod quietly, the effect was CRASH – 2, 3, 4 . . . later I added a groan on the fourth beat, CRASH, 2, 3, GROAN; CRASH, 2, 3, GROAN.

* Our Battery Commander.

Part Two orders

'Disciplinary action will be taken against other ranks responsible for the stamping and groaning on route marches.'

I noted Frangipani everywhere, but not yet in flower, magenta coloured Bougainvilleas were in full bloom. Towards evening the air filled with the cloying perfume of Jasmine, Belasarius was said to have placed one in his helmet at Tricaramaron saying, 'If I die, I will at least smell sweet ...' Generals! Going into battle? Then use Perfume of Jasmine! Hear what one General says:

General Montgomery: I use Jasmine – I couldn't have won El Alamein without it. Get some today.

Marches took us through timeless Arab villages, Rouiba, Ain-Taya, Fondouk, when we halted I'd try the Arab coffee; piping hot, sweet, delicious. I watched Gunner White sip the coffee then top it up with water! I explained the water was for clearing the palate. 'I thought it was for coolin' it down,' said the descendant of the Crusaders.

Local Arab. Nr Fondouk – Jan 20
'43

Lieutenant Joe Mostyn was Jewish, five foot six, on bad days five foot two, and, no matter how frequently he shaved, had a permanent blue chin; 'try shaving from the inside' I suggested. His forte was scrounging grub. One route march he bought a hundred eggs for twelve francs. Having no way of transporting them, he made us carry one in each hand till we reached Camp. Puzzled wayfarers watched as British soldiers marched by, clutching eggs accompanied by mass clucking. Water was rationed but we were on the sea. At day's end we plunged into the blue Med. I watched gunners, unfamiliar with salt water, try to get their soap to lather. 'Something wrong wiv it,' says Liddel. 'Nuffink can go wrong wiv soap,' replies Forrest, who plunges into a furious effort to prove his point. 'You're right,' he finally concedes. 'This soap is off.' NAAFI Managers tried to understand how some fifteen gunners all had soap that wouldn't lather. No one mentioned salt water, dutifully they exchanged the soaps. Next morning the soap lathered beautifully. 'This is better,' said Forrest. That evening, at swim parade, I watched Forrest and Liddel arguing about what had gone wrong with the soap since morning. We all bathed starkers, the lads gave wonderful displays of Military Tool-waving at passing ladies with cries of 'Vive le Sport' or 'Get in Knob its yer birthday.'

It was all good stuff and bore out Queen Victoria's belief that 'Salt Water has beneficial effects on the human body.' There were dreadful gunners who floated on their backs playing submarines. At the approaching of a maritime phallus, Gunner Devine shouted 'Achtung! Firen Torpedo!' and threw a pebble, and the hit 'periscope' would sink with a howl of pain. Another nasty trick was invented by Gunner Timms: Tie rock to piece of string, make noose at other end, next, dive under unsuspecting happily swimming gunner, slip noose over end of his Willie, let go rock; retire to safe distance. Mind you some gunners *liked* it. You can get used to anything I suppose.

We had received no mail. 'They've forgotten us! Out of sight out of mind!' says Gunner Woods scratching himself in bed.

'You're always moaning,' says 'Hooter' Price. 'I got

a wife and two kids, and I bet they haven't forgotten me.'

'With that bleedin' great nose, I don't suppose they can.'

'Look, a large nose is a sign of intelligence. The Duke of Wellington had one.'

'Yer, 'e 'ad one, but you look like you got two, and,' I added, 'how come you're only a bleedin' driver eh?'

'I chose to stay with the men,' said Price with great indignation. In the dark, a boot bounced off his nut.

One morning, on Part Two orders, 0800 hours: *'Gunner Milligan, S., Golding, Hart, E., Wenham, B., report to Sergeant Andrews for "Camouflage" course.'* This consisted of climbing over walls, ditches, fences, fag packets, in fact, anything. The course showed how it was possible to climb any tall obstruction. It became known as 'Leaping.' I wrote a letter home to my brother Desmond, explaining how Leaping could be done in civvy street.

Palm Trees and Vegetation near the head Cap Matifou Jan 1943

26

My dear Des,

In Africa we are all playing silly buggers. We are on a course teaching us how to 'Leap' anything that stands in our way. I think this could be introduced at home to encourage fitness among the War-time civilian population. For example 'Leaping Stones' could be installed in the home. The stone, about three feet high by two feet wide, could be cemented in all the doorways in the home, including one at the foot of the stairs.

A Leapo-meter is attached to the ankle of every member of the family, which records the number of leaps per person, per day. Those who show disinterest can have a small explosive charge fixed to the groin, which detonates should the person try climbing round the stone, this will cause many a smoke blackened crotch, but with our new spray-on 'Crotcho!' – a few squirts leaves the groins gleaming white, and free of fowl pest. Think of the enervating joys of the Leaping stones! Sunday morn – and the whole household rings with shouts of Hoi Hup! Ho la! Grannies, uncles, mothers, cripples all leaping merrily from one room to another for wartime England – ah, there's true patriotism! We have high hopes that more progressive young politicians with an eye to eliminating senile M.P.s, intend to have a 'Great Westminster Leaping Stone' that will be placed dead centre of the great entrance doors on opening day. Mr Churchill could start the leaping, those failing will of course be debarred. You can try and assist the failed member over the leaping stone by applying hot pokers to the seat, thus the smell of scorched flesh, burning hairs and screams, can bring a touch of colour to an otherwise dull wartime England. I don't know when I will post this letter, I might deliver it tomorrow by hand, ankle, foot and clenched elbow.

As ever,
Your loving brother
Terry.

To help kill boredom in the Camp I started a daily news bulletin posted outside my tent.

X Camp 201 PoW
MILLI-NEWS

Libya: *Last night, under cover of drunken singing, British Commandos with their teeth blacked out, raided an advance Italian Laundry, several vital laundry lists were captured, and a complete set of Marshall Gandolfo's underwear, which showed he was on the run.*

China: *Chinese troops are reported in the area with their eyes at the slope.*

Syria: *It is reported that Australian troops have taken Cascara. They are trying to keep it dark but it is leaking out in places and the troops are evacuating all along the line.*

Rome: *Il Duce told the Italian people not to worry about the outcome of the war. If they lost, he had relatives in Lyons Corner House, from whence he would run the Government in Exile.*

Local: *Sanitary Orderly Liddel takes pleasure in announcing his new luxury long drop Karzi.* Secluded surroundings, screened from the world's vulgar gaze by Hessian. Plentiful supply of Army Form Blank. Book now to avoid disappointment in the dysentery season.*

* From the Zulu word M'Karzi, meaning W.C.

'When are we going to be allowed into Algiers?' Says Gunner Edwards, who is cutting Gunner Knott's hair, and making his head look like a Mills grenade.

'They're frightened to let us in, we might get into the Kasbah and catch Syph.'

'That's all Cobblers, they're stoppin' us, so the officers can screw all the best birds first, that's yer Democracy for you,' says Gunner Thorpe, who is scraping his toe nails with a Jack-knife.

'You're talking balls. Just because you get first bash at a

French tart don't mean you're democratic! I mean shaggin' a bird is the same if you're a Commy or a Fascist, fucking is *real* democracy.'

A solemn cheer greeted this. 'Look, if none of us ever had a screw again we've had enough hoggins in Bexhill to last forever.' Cries of 'No! Resign!'

'A man can never have enough hoggins, a good shag clears the custard,' said Gunner Balfour as he wrote a tender love letter off to his wife.

Gunner Maunders, his feet reeking, sits up in his bed. 'They say French tarts can shag all night on one dinner.'

'That's right,' says Lance Bombardier Denning, 'they can shag around the clock, in any position.'

'Good,' says Gunner Knott. 'From now on I'm going to shag laying down, no more bangin' away standin' in Bexhill doorways in the shape of a cripple.' Cries of 'Knee trembler.'

Discussions on sex took up large portions of gunners' working hours. The nearest they got to it was the Estaminet at Jean Bart, a quarter of a mile from the Camp. There, apart from the booze, was a barmaid whose bulging bosoms floated along the top of the bar with never less than a hundred pairs of eyes to help them on their way. Many hot-blooded gunners ruptured themselves just staring. 'Try only looking at one at a time,' I advised them. There was no shortage of alcohol. We guzzled muscatel, about eighty per cent proof, the real proof was hundred per cent stoned gunners, spark out in the gutters. Those who could stagger would go down to the beach. Naked, we'd sit waist deep in the water, to sober up. One such night, (Jan. 19th 1943) the port of Algiers had a 'sudden attack of air raid,' soon the sky was a mass of exploding shells, flaming onions and searchlights.

We sat and enjoyed it. 'It's lovely,' said Edgington. 'Yesh, it's slouvely,' I agreed. Gunner Roberts took from the waters to don his steel helmet.

'What German is going to by-pass Algiers to bomb you,' says Edgington.

'They say on a moonlit night an airman can see a bald head from 20,000 feet,' said Roberts. 'You haven't got a bald head,' says I. 'I'm not waiting till the last minute,' says

Anti-aircraft fire at night. Algiers

Roberts. I got back to the beach and returned with fags.

'Ta,' said Edgington, 'nothing like wet cigarettes covered in bloody sand.'

We sat silent. Edgington spoke. 'Milligan? See if your aeroplane curse still works.' I stood up. I waited till a German plane was caught in a searchlight, then shouted 'I hope you bloody well crash.' Nothing happened.

'Perhaps it's a deaf pilot,' said Edgington.

'I HOPE YOU BLOODY CRASHHHHH.'

'We're too far away,' said Edgington.

'Let's forget it.'

'Forget what?' he said.

'See?' I said, 'you've forgotten it already.' He too, forgetting, lay back and disappeared below the surface. He reappeared spluttering. 'This water's unreliable,' he said. We dressed and started to wander back. It was dark. Being nyctalopic* I always carried a torch. Suddenly in the beam hopped an animal,

* Find out like I did.

'I hope you bloody well crash' I said

'Look,' I said, 'it's a jerboa!'

'Jerboa my arse, that's a kangaroo,' says Forrest.

'What's a kangeroo doing in Africa?'

'There's no such animal, Milligan,' says Edgington, 'you made the word up.'

'On the bible it's true!'

'Bible? You're agnostic!'

'O.K. I swear on Tiger Tim's Weekly.'

'Halt, who goes there?' came the midnight challenge.

'Hitler,' I said.

'You can't be! He came in ten minutes ago.'

'We don't know who we are, we're Military Amnesiacs Anonymous.'

'What's the password?'

'We give up, what is the password?'

'I'm waiting,' said the sentry.

'So are we . . . gi's a clue.'

'The clue is, what's the password?'

'Just a minute,' says Edgington, 'I've got it written here on a piece of paper . . . Ahhhh! the word is "Fish".'

'That was last night.'

'Chips?'

'No.'

'Shirley Temple.'

'I don't know why they put me on sentry duty,' said the demoralised sentry. 'There's seventy blokes come in in the last two hours and not one bugger remembered the word. It's a waste of bloody time. Sod Churchill.' We gave him a rousing cheer and he let us in.

January the 23rd: Bombardier Harry Baum, nicknamed 'Hairy Bum,' told us 'You lot are to be allowed into Algiers and let loose on the unsuspecting women therein. The Passion Wagon leaves at 13.30 hours, and you will all be back at 23.59, like all gude little Cinderellas.' Fly buttons flew in all directions.

We set about cleaning up. Boots were boned, web belts scrubbed, brass polished and trousers creased. It made little difference, we still looked like sacks of shit tied up in the middle. A three tonner full of sexual tension, rattled us to Algiers Docks. Most others were looking for Women and Booze. Not Gunner Milligan, I was a good Catholic boy, I didn't frequent brothels.

No, all I did was walk round with a permanent erection shoutin 'Mercy!', in any case, I was in the company of 'Mother Superior Edgington,' who shunned such practices. Was he not the one who threw his army issue contraceptive into the sea where it was later sunk by naval gun fire? So we entered Algiers, with pure minds, and the sun glinting on the Brylcream running down our necks. We were joined by Bdr Spike Deans and Gunner Shapiro. Along the main tree-lined Rue d'Isly, we entered a small café, 'Le Del Monico.' 'That means "The Del Monico",' I explained. Inside we were shown to a table by an attractive French waitress. We perused the menu.

MENU
Moules Mariniere
Homus
Spigola al Forno
Sole Nicoise
Scampi Provencale
Poulet Roti
Carre d'Agnau
Courgettes

'Eggs and chips four times,' we said. 'Make mine Kosher,' added Shapiro.

'There's no such thing as Jewish Chicken,' I said.

'And I'll tell you why,' said Shapiro, 'there's no money in it.' The eggs arrived sizzling in round copper dishes. 'Where's the chips?' says Shapiro. 'She's forgotten the chips.'

'Don't be bloody ignorant,' rebukes Edgington, 'in French cooking le chips are served separate! Patience!' So we sat in patience. We sat a long time in patience. She *had* forgotten 'le chips.' The mistake rectified, we ate the meal with quaffs of Thibar Rosé.

'You'd never think there was a war on,' said Dean.

'*I* think there's a war on,' said Shapiro.

'I notice,' said Edgington, 'you dip your chip into the yolk first.'

'True,' I said. 'I cannot tell a lie.' We finished the meal.

'What now?' says Milligan.

'Let's go to the pictures,' says Shapiro.

'PICTURES? We come all the way from England to Africa and you want to go to the bloody PICTURES?'

'I like the pictures,' he says, 'they make me forget.'

'Forget what?'

'I can't remember.'

We decided to wander through Algiers, it was amazing how boring it could be. 'Isn't this the place where Charles Boyer screwed Hedy Lamarr?' said Deans. 'Yes,' I said. 'I'm not surprised,' said Edgington, 'there's nothing else to do.' We followed signs 'THIS WAY TO WVS CANTEEN, ALLIED TROOPS WELCOME.' The building looked like a warehouse. We went in. It was a warehouse. Tables and chairs were spread around a massive hall-like room. Behind tea-bearing tables were middle-aged English ladies who also looked like warehouses, they obviously thought being in Algiers was 'naughty.' We drank piss poor tea and ate buns made of leather.

Edgington was already slumped over a desk, dashing off a 'Darling-I-love-you-I-always-do-you-love-me' etc. etc. standard soldier's letter for the relief of sexual tension, pausing only to hit his re-occurring erection with an ink well. I used to write to several birds, but hadn't realised my letters were getting stereotyped until one replied 'Darling, Thank you for your circular . . .' Edgington wrote reams, average letter twenty pages. He was the most pure of gunners and faithful to his sweetheart. Mind you he missed a lot of fun and his machinery got very rusty. I woke Shapiro. 'Dreaming of the Promised Land?' I said. 'No, I was dreaming of East Finchley, it's cheaper there,' he said yawning. Evening; we sauntered out into the main Boulevard. All the prettiest French birds were out, chaperoned by what looked like the Mafia and an occasional Quasimodo. We promenaded up and down. 'We can get all this bloody route marching at camp,' said Shapiro, 'let's lie down.' We repaired to a street café 'quatre verres cognac' I said to a waiter. 'Never mind all that crap,' he said, 'what do you want to drink?' The brandy arrived.

'Here's to a safe war,' said Dean, and spilled the lot over his jacket. We downed several brandies in the next hour, and all became decidedly unsafe. Shapiro dozed off. 'He's not asleep,' said Edgington, 'it's a Jewish ruse, the next round's his!' 'Wake up Shap,' I said, 'your turn to pay.' 'You're a Fascist,' said Shapiro, unchaining his wallet. The sun was setting, so were my legs. No one could remember the way. 'Follow me,' said Edgington. Twenty minutes later we stopped. '*Now* do you know where you are?'

34

'It's the café we left twenty minutes ago.'

'See?' he said, 'let's go in.'

By 23.15 hours we were all in the Passion Waggon. The noise was incredible, talking, singing, farting, laughing, vomiting. Versatility was going to win us the war. It was horrible, but, there was a kind of mad strange poetry to it, that is, ask any one why they were like they were at that moment and they'd have a rational answer.

Drunks being loaded into 'Passion Waggon' after first visit to Algiers

An hour later we settled in our beds, listening to the lurid exploits of Driver 'Plunger' Bailey, 'Plunger' because he had a prick the size and shape of a sink pump. He had entered the forbidden Kasbah in the search of his 'hoggins' and gained entrance to an Arab brothel, 'They wouldn't let me in till I took me boots off,' he said. He had been shown a room where a naked Arab girl had entertained him with a belly dance, feeling he should reciprocate he sang her a chorus of 'The

Lambeth Walk' and then 'got stuck up her.' From now on, all my illusions of the Arabian Nights were dead.

January the 27th 1943: The services of the Battery Band were called for. 'There's ten acts on the bill and we'd like yeow to do a twurn!' said the District Entertainments Officer. He had a very high effeminate voice. 'I used to be counter-tenor at the Gwarden,' he said. 'It must have been Welwyn Garden,' whispered Edge. That evening, a highly polished staff car calls for us. 'Don't touch it,' I cautioned, 'it's a trap, it's only for our instruments, we're supposed to run alongside.' We were driven at great speed to a massive French Colonial Opera House where at one time, massive French colonials sang. A sweating Sergeant was waiting,

'Ah,' he said with obvious relief. 'I'm Sergeant Hope.'

'What a good memory you've got,' I said.

'I'm the compère. You are the Royal Artillery Orchestra?'

'Yes,' I said.

'Where's the rest of you?'

'This is all there is of me, I'm considered complete by the M.O.'

'We had been expecting a full Orchestra.'

'We are full – we just had dinner.'

'That will do,' he said leading us to the wings.

On stage an Army P.T. Instructor was doing a series of hand stands, leaps, and somersaults, the conclusion of each trick was standing to attention and saluting. 'You don't salute without yer 'at on, cunt,' said a voice from the Khaki rabble. Sgt Hope took down details of our 'act.'

'Name?'

'Milligan.'

'Rank?'

'Gunner.'

'Regiment?'

'I'm sorry,' I said, 'under the Geneva Convention of 1921 all I need give is my name, rank and number.'

'Look son, I've had a bloody awful day, I'm at the end of my tether,' he said. 'Save the jokes for the stage, I was told you were a twenty piece Regimental Orchestra and you were

36

going to play Elgar's Pomp and Circumstances,' he walked away holding his head.

The P.T. Sergeant finished his leaping act, and was given a reception that he had never had before or since. He came into the wings grinning with triumph. 'I think I'll turn pro after the war,' he triumphed. The next time I saw him was 1951, he was a furniture remover in Peckham. 'Changed your mind?' I said. He threw a cupboard at me. The worried compère was now the other side of the curtain saying 'Thank you, the next act is – er – the 19th "Battalion", Royal Artillery Dance Band, under its – er – conductor Gunner Spine Millington!' Behind the curtain we were rupturing ourselves trying to get a massive French colonial piano on the stage. I shouted 'We're not bloody well ready.' 'Well,' said the sweating Sergeant, 'as you can hear they're not quite bloody well ready yet ha-ha but – er – they ha-ha – er – won't be long now, and then—' he put his head through the curtain. 'Hurry up for Christ's sake!' 'Keep ad libbing,' I said, 'you're a natural.' He continued 'Well, they're – er – nearly – er – not quite – ready, ha-ha and soon we'll be . . .' Not waiting for him to finish, we launched into our up tempo signature tune, 'The Boys From Battery D', which Harry Edgington had written.

> We're the boys from Battery D
> Four Boys from Battery D
> We make a rhythmic noise
> We give you dancing joys
> And sing the latest melody.
>
> Now we make the darndest sounds
> As we send you Truckin' on down
> And if it's sweet or hot
> We give it all we've got
> And boy! we got enough to go around.
>
> We'll set your feet tapping with a quick step
> We've a waltz that'll make you sigh
> And then the tempo we've got
> For a slow fox-trop
> Would make a wallflower wanna try.

37

Come on along you he and she
It's the dancers jamboree
Come on and take a chance
Come on and have a dance
To the band of Battery D.

*My life long pal Harry
Edgington playing an 88
mm Piano in action, at the
same time inflating his head*

Not exactly Cole Porter, but we weren't getting his kind of
money. To our amazement we got an ovation. Three more
jazz numbers and they wouldn't let us go, to cool them off I
got Doug Kidgell our drummer to sing Toselli's Serenade.
When he came to the line:

'Deep in my heart there is Rapture'

forgetfully we sang our customary version:

'Deep in my guts I've got Rupture
But for that dear
I'd have upped yer.'

We realised our mistake too late, and a great roar of
laughter stopped the song in its tracks. We finished up with
me impersonating Louis Armstrong doing The St Louis

Blues, and took unending curtain calls. Old soldiers reading this may remember that occasion.

Driving back in the staff car, we sat silent in the aura of our unexpected success. To our left the Bay of Algiers was bathed in moonlight. 'I never dreamed,' said Harry, 'that one day, I would be driven along the Bay of Algiers by moonlight.' 'Didn't you?' I said, 'the first time I saw you I said "one day that man is going to be driven along the Bay of Algiers by moonlight".'

'You're asking for a thud up the hooter,' he said.

'No I wasn't! What I said was, "the first time I saw you I . . ."'

'All right Milligan, stick this in yer dinner manglers.' He gave me a cigarette. Old sweats will shudder and fall faint when I mention the brand, 'V's'! They had appeared in our rations when we landed in Algiers. 'This is,' I said, 'living proof that the British soldier will smoke shit, and that goes from Sanitary Orderly Geordie Liddel to General Alexander.' Alf Fildes, our guitarist, disagreed. 'Liddel, yes, he lives near it, he'd smoke shit, yes, but I bet a bloke like Alexander wouldn't wear it.' There followed a classical argument on smoking shit, that resolved in the agreement that General Alexander *would* smoke shit provided it was offered him by the King. The story went round that 'V's' were India's contribution to the war. Churchill asked Ghandi if there was a natural commodity that was going to waste, and Ghandi said 'Yes, we got plenty of cows' shit.' 'Right,' said Churchill, 'we're sending you a million rupees to turn it into tobacco.' Two years went by, Churchill, anxious for news, phones Ghandi:

CHURCHILL: Ghandi? How's the Ersatz tobacco coming along?

GHANDI: All right but we need more money.

CHURCHILL: Good God, you've had a million!

GHANDI: Yes, you see, so far it *looks* like tobacco – it *smokes* like tobacco – but –

CHURCHILL: But what?

GHANDHI: It still smells like shit.

The long haul to the front

One day, there was the long awaited news on the notice board.

0600 11 FEB. 1943. Regiment will prepare to move etc. etc.

Great excitement, packing, renewing kit, selling kit, buying fruit for the journey, writing 'Farewell for ever' etc. to sweethearts, etc. The day before the move I developed toothache. It started at two in the morning, the pain shot up my head down the back of my neck, disappeared down my spine then reappeared in my chest sideways up the tent pole. How could one tiny hole neutralise a whole man? Will-power! *That* would stop it. I did will-power till three o'clock. It got worse. Old wives' recipe! Stuff tobacco into the cavity. I lit the lamp. Edgington woke, he saw what appeared to be Gunner Milligan splitting open cigarettes and poking the tobacco down his throat. 'Look mate,' he said, 'you're supposed to smoke 'em.'

Next morning, I drove to the Dental Surgery, in a villa on the sea at Cap Matifou. The dentist, a young fair-haired Captain sat me in the chair, and drove his prodder down till it got through to the collar bone.

'OWWWWWWWWWWWWWWWWWWWWWWW Sir,' I said.

'You scream very well.'

'Yes sir, I'm practising for the front line.'

I drove back with the left side of my face frozen dead. You may ask, what use is half a frozen face? Well, it keeps longer. To this day, the left side of my face is two hours younger than the right. We were to fill in our wills in the back of our Army Pay Books. I had no possessions, no money, two cheap fifty shilling suits, a second-hand evening dress, a few Marks and Spencer shirts, and a mess of ragged underwear. My trumpet was my only bounty, so I wrote 'I leave my trumpet to my mother and the H.P. payments to my father.' Others made lavish entries, Gunner White 'I leave my Gas Stove to the Sgt Major,' etc. To some it wasn't funny. Reg Griffin said 'When millions of perfectly healthy young men have to make their wills out, there's something nasty going on in the world.'

'This tea tastes funny,' I said.

'It's Bromide,' said Gunner Devine. 'It stops you havin' improper thoughts while you're in action and causing you to lose your aim.'

Gunner James Patrick Devine – one of the great characters of the Battery

'Wot you sayin'?' says Gunner Forrest (who was very dim).

'Wot I'm sayin',' says Devine, 'is that Bromide stops you getting randy when there is no women about to be the recipient of your desires.' The Bromide had some effect, the Onanists were much less active and we all got to sleep earlier. Gunner Moffat didn't like Bromide, he was a Christian Science Monitor, he stopped drinking tea in case it 'interferes with my manhood.' Bombardier Dean told him it was also in the food. So he stopped eating and lived on Arab fruits, as a result he got galloping dysentery and went down to seven stone before he was weaned back to Bully Beef. I don't think the Bromide had any lasting effect, the only way to stop a British soldier feeling randy is to load Bromide into a 300 lb. shell and fire it at him from the waist down.

Dawn, February the 11th 1943. Yawning, I threw back the tent flap and felt the chill air run over me in the pre-dawn light, I hadn't been able to sleep, the excitement of the coming adventure had got me. I had risen first, dressed and started packing my kit. As the morning grew my comrades started to stir, the odd voice commenced to break the silence in the camp. After breakfast I loaded my kit onto the Humber Snipe Wireless Truck.

At 8.30 a.m. the transport of the Regiment was lined up pointing due East. Edgington, late as usual, was swearing,

'If I have to pack this bloody kit once more I'll – I'll become affiliated to the Swonnicles.'

'You don't mean that dark beauteous gunner' I said wiggling me fingers.

His kit bag looked as though he had a dismantled gasometer inside. A squadron of Bell Airacobras roared over.

'I hope you bloody well crash' I shouted instantly.

'Any luck?' said Harry.

'No.'

'Your power is waning.'

'Rubbish! I've got the lowest wain-fall in the Battery.'

'Get out before I laugh,' said Harry pointing upwards.

Driver Shepherd and I had been detailed to drive Lt Budden, in the Wireless Truck. We had been standing by vehicles for an hour and nothing had happened but it happened frequently. Despatch Riders raced up and down the column shouting 'Fuck everybody' but that was all. We

Humber Snipe Wireless Truck

started to brew tea, when Lt Budden's Iron Frame Glasses appear round the truck, 'Look damn you! You're supposed to be standing by your vehicles.'

'Sorry sir, I'll say three Hail Marys.'

'Give me a cup and I'll say no more about it,' he said producing a mug from behind his back.

Lt Budden flags down a D.R. 'What's the hold up?'

'I'll tell you sir. I'm the D.R. who follows the D.R. in front with a message that cancels out his message.'

A cloud of dust is approaching at high speed. From its nucleus formidable swearing is issuing. It's our Signal Sergeant Dawson, 'Get mounted, we're off,' it bellows as it goes down the line, followed by mocking cheers. I jump in, engines are coming to life, the hood is rolled back so Budden can stand Caesar-like in the passenger seat. Shouts are heard above the sound of the engines revving. 'Right Milligan,' says Lt Budden. 'World War Two at 25 m.p.h.' He looked back at the long line of vehicles. 'My God, what a target for the Luftwaffe.'

'Don't worry sir, I have a verbal anti-aircraft curse, that brings down planes.'

'Keep talking Milligan. I think I can get you out on Mental Grounds.'

'That's how I got in, sir.'

'Didn't we all.'

There was a throttle on the steering column, I set it to a steady twenty m.p.h.

'I said twenty-five,' said Budden.

'Trying to economise, sir. The slower we go chances are by the time we get there it might be all over.'

'Oh it *will* be all over Milligan,' he said, 'all over bloody Africa.'

We rolled along comfortably, the sun warm, scenery magnificent. We stopped for ten minutes every two hours to stretch legs. I didn't stretch mine as they seem to be long enough. At every halt, Arabs materialised from nowhere bearing eggs, dates, and some long black things that looked like petrified eels or models of 'Plunger' Bailey's weapon.

We pressed on, crossing the River Isser, a thick, brown,

tortuous winding affair flowing very fast, it kept company with us until we reached the village of Les Isser, a cluster of mud buildings. Outside a seedy white Gendarmerie, an un-shaven seedy off-white gendarme slumbered in a chair. 'He's pretending there isn't a war on,' said Mr Budden. I shouted 'Ai Meisu! le Gendarme? Où est la Guerre Mondiale Nombre Deux?'

He pointed up the road. 'Avante siese mille kilo.' He grinned and fell back to sleep.

19 Battery men on their march to the Front being accosted by consenting French Vichy Seamen

Here is an excerpt from Major Chater Jack's letter of the time:

'Here I sit in a truck by the road side, the country is all covered with olive trees, Caroo Beans and Alloes, there are snow capped mountains in the distances and a deep turbid muddy river flowing through the centre of a broad fertile valley . . . What growing country this is! There have been no vineyards for a long time; a few orange groves but the crop is nearly over. Mostly Arabs about, herding flocks of goats, some cattle, some French people in the first few days, but now an Italian strain is showing.'

A lonely French Barracks in Regents Park

CHAS. DE GAULLE: I am France, Zear iss no osaire leader. France ees de Gaulle, de Gaulle ees France! (he sings the Marseillaise)

GUNNER: Fer Christ sake go to kip.

DE GAULLE: How can I kip ven I zer leader of France, only 'ave ten francs and ze arse out of my trousers!

GUNNER: It's yer own bleedin' fault, you shouldn't be rude to Churchill.

DE GAULLE: Churchill! zat man! he is calling me a 'Froggie', sometimes he says I am Jewish!

CHURCHILL: You must be the Froggie Froggie Jew!

Funny, I never knew the Major was suffering from Italian strain. 1300 hours. Arrived village of Camp du Marechal. (Q.) What 'Marechal' was it named after? (A.) 'It's had a railway siding' said Edgington, 'so it must be (all together) Marechal Yard!' 'Three out of ten,' I said. We sat down to eat 'the unexpired portion of our rations,' 'unexpired' being a piece of bully beef that is gradually dying for its country. I grabbed my throat, staggered round gasping 'This bully's been poisoned with food Ahhhh!' and fell to the ground.

'Bury me up a tree,' I said.

'You bloody fool,' said Edge, 'why?'

'After I die I want people to look up to me.'

'Three out of ten,' he said placing one finger in his ear.

Lunch over and on to battle. Above, the sky was cobalt, cloudless, the Djebels stood out stark blue-grey in the clear light. On our left, the silt laden waters of the Sebaou thundered in a titanic gorge on its way to the Mediterranean. Donkeys with riders perched on their haunches were passing by and pulling more donkeys almost lost to view under sacks of produce. The animals looked in a sorry state, but then so did the Arabs. We were nearing a large town with the champagne name 'Tizi Ouzou!' 'What's that mean?' asked student of Arabic, Gunner White.

'It's an ancient Arab proverb,' I said.

'No it isn't,' he said, 'it's a wog town.'

'Let me explain, it means the Shadow of the Razor falls directly under the earole of Mahomet, but it's cheaper by the pound.'

'Git,' said Chalky in Bradford accents, 'Where do you think up all that bloody crap?'

'Any open space,' I said. Outside Tizi Ouzou, we pulled off the road among groves of orange trees. That night I slept Al Fresco, and there's nothing better, except sleeping Al Jolson.

Next day, according to my diary, I sat in the back of the truck with a 'Huge pink idiot youth from Egham', who I don't seem to be able to recall. Egham yes, him *no*, but Egham yes. Perhaps I was sitting in the back with a huge pink Egham? I passed the time testing the wireless set, when I got

Part of the Regimental Convoy on its way to the front – Jan. 1943

'This is the Allied Forces Network, Algeria' a stentorian American voice said 'Here for your listening pleasure is Tommy Dorsey and his Orchestra.' Great! I listened all day. I lit up a cigarette, now this was more like war.

A sign, Sik-en-Meadou, 'Sir,' I called to Budden, 'We've just passed a sign saying someone's been Sick-in-the-Meadow'; there was no reply, just silence, but dear reader, it was a *commissioned* officer's silence, of course, if you were a Brigadier you could command a brigade of silence, there was no end to it. I could feel it getting chilly at nights and made a mental note where my balaclava was . . . In the drawer of a cupboard in 50 Riseldine Road, Brockley, S.E.26. 'You'll never need woollens in Africa,' my father had said. The movement of the truck had lulled huge pink faced idiot from Egham to sleep. When we staged for the night I woke him up.

'Where are we?' he said.

'Africa,' I replied.

'Oh,' he said, 'I thought it was Egham.' What he needed was a direct hit.

The Arabs of this village looked better off than the plain Arabs. (Two plain Arabs and one with chocolate sauce please.)

Battery Diary:

'Feb. 11 1943. Staged Beni Mansour.'

If brevity is the soul of wit this diary was written by Oscar Wilde.

My Diary:

Found a tree with heavy foliage to keep off the dew and, if needs be, Oscar Wilde.

I placed my bed head towards the trunk between radiating roots. Radiating out from the tree are Gunners Edgington, Tume, White, Shepherd, total financial holdings – 8 shillings. The night closed in, there was an almighty silence, a distant barking dog became a major sound. The soldiers grew still. There was a loud painful yell. 'Fire bug' Bennett had dozed off with a cigarette on and set himself and his bedding alight for the umpteenth time. His blankets looked like early piano rolls. Peace was restored, the silence broken only by the slow tramping of the picket. Each time he passed, puns from recumbent soldiers 'You'll never get well if you pick-it,' or 'Keep going there's a bone in the cookhouse for you.' He silenced us with one threat 'You've had your fun and I'll have mine, tomorrow morning at *five o'clock*, when you will have an accidental rude awakening with my boot up your nose.'

Somewhere a donkey was braying into the darkness. 'Coming Mother,' said Gunner White.

Gunners bringing Porridge into action against German Sausages

8.00 Feb. 11: Breakfast, what's this? PORRIDGE! It *was* PORRIDGE, watery grey, *but porridge*. So the porridge convoys *were* getting through. Now this was better, this was more like the suffering we are supposed to have in wars. Porridge! We paraded at our vehicles, small arms inspection, check on ammunition then off again and Porridge.

We were climbing steadily all day, jagged peaks three and four thousand feet ranged on either side. From Major Chater Jack's diary of 12 Feb. mid-day:

'. . . *very cold just now as we are high up in the mountains and I have just halted the column for half an hour. It is still a stiff pull for our vehicles. We climbed up and up following bend after hairpin bend, through pinewoods until we reached the open flat plain between the mountaintops. It is across this plain we are now travelling . . .*'

Twixt Tizi Ouzou and Beni Mansour we passed mountains each side of 8,000 feet, and numerous rock-hewn tunnels.

'Attention! Rallientair!' signs appeared frequently. We saw camel trains all laden with goods. They followed ancient camel tracks two or three hundred feet above us, moving

Hitlergram No. 697312

The scene, a glittering affair in a German NAAFI.
The band under General Glen von Miller.

HITLER: Ach Meiner beautiful may I have zer Collapse of France Waltz with you?

GUNNER MILLIGAN: Thank you!

HITLER: You dance beautifully but, IT IS NOT GOOD ENOUGH FOR ZER FÜHRER!

PETAIN: Pardonnez-moi Hitler. This is a Vichy excuse me one step.

HITLER: Take zis olf French Twit outside and shoot him! Now what is your name?

GUNNER MILLIGAN: Gunner Milligan.

HITLER: Gunter Milligan? Vere haff I hears zat name before?

ME: I give up. Where have you heard that name before?

HITLER: Playing hard to get, hein? Take this woman out and shoot him.

slowly with a dignity no civilization had managed to speed up. At sundown the Arabs turned towards Mecca to carry out their devotions, a religious people, more than I could say for our lot, the only time *they* knelt was to pick up money.

Feb. 12th: approaching Setif : A large French colonial town. We passed fifty sweating, spotty, French civilians being drilled by a Legion Sergeant. 'Don't look!' I said. 'It might be contagious!' A line of black clad Arab ladies carrying pitchers moved liquidly by. 'You'd think their old man would buy 'em a suitcase,' said Chalky White.

'How you gonna carry bloody water in a suitcase?'

'Look, I just *think* of the ideas, it's up to the wogs to make 'em work.'

As we entered this dusty town the French Mayor came out and greeted us with a huge stomach, sweat, a speech and numerous gesticulations. Major Chater Jack's reply was to the point.

'Merci, bon chance, and Vive la France.'

'I suppose there'll be a grand ball at Versailles tonight,' said Edgington.

We bivouacked just outside Setif. We'd had a good day buying Arab supplies, eggs, potatoes and chickens, so a great meal was in the offing. We backed two wireless trucks together, threw a blanket over the join, inside we rigged an inspection light, and picked up BBC on the set. The food came steaming in the chilly night air as I uncorked the Vin Rosé. I can still see the scene, the young faces, poised eagerly over the food, all silent save the odd 'Cor lovely' and the clank of forks on mess tins. We listened to the news.

'I think it will be over by Christmas,' said White.

'You said that last year, *and* the year before.'

'I'm playing the waiting game,' says White. 'But this time,' he held up his fork to emphasize a point, like lightning, I snatched it from his hand, scooped a mouthful of egg from his mess tin and said 'You're right! By the taste of that egg it will definitely be over this year.' I looked at the engraving on the fork 'Devonshire Hotel. Bexhill.'

Bdr 'Spike' Deans with Arab chicken purchased by wayside

'Give it here,' snatched White. 'It's a souvenir of our last supper in Bexhill.'

'Last supper?' said Edgington. 'If you were at the last supper, Jesus must have kept his bloody mess tins on a chain.'

'Arrest that man,' says White, 'boil his balls in syrup and serve when cool.'

We drained the last of the wine, smoked, turned in, turned off. It was a hunter's moon, so we went to sleep shouting 'Tally Ho!'

Feb. 13th 1943. This morning, tired of those coughing, scratching Reveilles, I took my trumpet and blew a swing bugle call. Chalky White appeared from under a blanket with a severe attack of face and eyes with blood filled canals. 'Whose bloody side are you on!' he groaned. Odd silent soldiers, hands in pockets, eating utensils tucked under arms were making their way to the Field Kitchen. Our Cook, Gunner May, a dapper lad with curly black hair and Ronald Colman moustache was doling out Porridge. He spoke with a very posh voice and Porridge.

'Where'd you get that accent Ronnie?' asked Gunner Devine.

'Eton old sausage.'

'Well I'd stop eatin' old sausages,' says Devine.

With a flick of the wrist, May sent a spoonful of Porridge into Devine's eye. 'Good for night blindness,' he says ducking a mug of tea.

From Setif the road to the front ran fairly straight. During a halt, along comes a pregnant American staff car that gave birth to an American called Eisenhower. The driver was a tall girl with a Veronica Lake hair-do. Eisenhower approached and spoke to, – I can't remember who, – but I recall him saying 'What kind of cannons are these?' (Cannons!? CANNONS!? That's like calling the H.M.S. *Ark Royal* a boat.) Eisenhower got back in the car, struck his head on the roof, said 'Oh Fuck' and left. He had shaken hands with Sergeant Mick Ryan who didn't know *who* he was. Ryan! Oh what a ruffian that man was! One night, back at Bexhill, he made for the fish and chip shop, as he reached the door the proprietor closed it.

'Sorry,' said the proprietor, 'we're closed.'

'No, you're bloody not,' said Ryan, punched through the glass door and laid him out.

18.00 hours o'clock: Observed squadron of Boston bombers flying very high headed towards the front. These days the sound of any plane made one jumpy. Since leaving Camp trucks and lorries had passed us taking mail etc. and supplies up front. This day a truck had arrived with *our* MAIL! 'Gunner Milligan?' shouted Bombardier Marsden. I ran fifty yards to him – 'Yes Bom?' 'No mail for you!' he told me gleefully. Bastard! I was shattered. What were all those women I had been sleeping with back home doing? I mean, now I'd gone, they'd have time on their hands! But worst there was no mail from Lily or Louise. First Lily! (MILLIGAN TELLS ALL. HIS LOVES, HIS DESIRES, HIS SECRET SEXUAL CODES, HIS OWN RECEIPT* FOR APHRODISIACS, TAKE SIX HUNDRED OYSTERS AND PORRIDGE ... AND READ IT ALL IN THE SUN!) It was 1936. I was aged seventeen, smothered in pimples, even my suit had them. I worked in S. Strakers of Queen Victoria Street. My pay was 13s a week. After the train fare from Honor Oak Park to London Bridge it left 7s and 6,000 pimples. Standing on Platform One of an evening, waiting for the six fifteen, a small crowd of casual acquaintances would congregate. London Bridge Station, grim, grey, like a mighty iron mangle that squeezed people through its rollers into compartments. Yet, I fell in love there, (Third Class) Lily! She was about five foot six. Delightfully shaped, dark hair, brown doe-like eyes, a funny nose and slim legs. But I wasn't interested. I was after a girl with green eyes and red hair with fat legs who wore an imitation leopard skin coat, but! Lily fancied me, she made it a point, like General Sherman, of being there 'firstust with the mostest.' The first time we met I was running along the platform to get a seat up front, in comes Lily, I say 'Take my seat.' 'No,' she smiles 'I'll sit on your lap.' She did, very disturbing for a young man brought up on curry, Cod Liver Oil and Keplers Malt. The relationship developed rapidly, and so did I. We fell madly in love. She wanted to get married, on 13s a week

---

* YES – A RECEIPT NOT A RECIPE. You see I made the stuff, but I always got a signature for it.

I couldn't. 13 shillings? We'd have to spend our honeymoon on a tram. Marriage? I was so innocent I had no idea how the sex act was performed. When a bloke said 'You get across a woman' I thought you laid on the woman crosswise making a Crucifix. I was seventeen, stupid, and a Roman Catholic. Any Questions? I had to learn the hard way – Braille! Of course I wanted sex. God! how clumsy I must have been. Finally after three years being fed up with waiting, she went off with some red headed twit called 'Roddy'. As far as she was concerned it was over. Not for me. Brought up on silent films with a romantic Irish father who told me I was descended from the Kings of Connaught, I played out the scene of the rejected lover. Sitting on a bench in Ladywell Recreation Ground, with a quarter of jelly babies, I would slump in the corner of the benches in a series of 'scorned attitudes' hoping she would come looking for me, like James Cagney in Shanghai Lil. I would do anything up to twenty-seven dejected poses a night, before the Park Keeper threw me out. What I needed was consolation. All my mother gave me was Weetabix. Playing local dances, I would buy ginger ale, disguise it in a whisky glass hoping she would see me taking gulps in between trumpet solos, pretending I was drunk. I was now Robert Taylor. I would play sobbing trumpet choruses until even the Jews would shout 'Stop! Enough is enough.' I would wait at night on the opposite side to her house, with my Marks and Spencer's mackintosh (5s 3d in a sale) coat collar up, making sure when she came home with the new boyfriend, I would be standing under the gas lamp, smoking a cigarette. When they arrived, I would throw down the cigarette, stamp on it, place my hands in my pockets then walk away whistling Bing Crosby's 'The Thrill is Gone'. I did that every night of December. I got pneumonia. Just what I wanted! I wrote and told her I was dying! She sent me a get well card. I thought, one evening I would throw myself from the bandstand and crash at the feet of her and her partner. Before I could, she moved her dancing habitat elsewhere. On the night I planned it, I sat sweating, finally I had to go to the Gents and remove the padding stuffed up the front of my shirt to take the shock of the fall.

She met someone with a car, I used to give chase, shouting threats. After a year of this I'd had the shoes resoled fifty times, chased the car 1,073 miles, lost hope and had calves like Nureyev, but, I imagined, like Camille, she would return one winter's night to die in my arms at 50 Riseldine Road, Brockley Rise, S.E.26. I'd offer her Champagne (Ovaltine), she would ask me to play 'Honeysuckle Rose' on my trumpet and then die. It didn't happen. And not only did it not happen, here I was by the roadside of some bloody wog village in Africa and she hadn't even bothered to write to me. But chum! Living in hope is no reason to go without. I mean, what's wrong with part-time love affairs which included night occupations from the waist down? I mean, I had to keep fit. To this end I let other women into my life. I was good looking so I went in at the deep end.

There was lovely Junoesque Ivy, her sister Magda, then her *married* sister, Eileen! Ivy had taught me how, and from then on there was no stopping me. I had to go on to vitamin pills. There was Dot on One Tree Hill, Brockley Doris who was to get married on the morrow, Deptford Flo, Miss MacCafferty of Lewisham Hospital. Once in uniform I ran into a spate of affairs. Oh Louise! Louise! Louise!

So no mail. 'Cheer up,' said Gunner Forester, 'You can read my letter, my wife's pissed off with a Polish Pilot.'

'With eyesight like that, how did he become a pilot?' I said.

Hitlergram No. 27

ADOLPH HITLER: You realize soon zer Englishers people will be *crushed*!

ME: It must be rush hour.

ADOLPH HITLER: Zere is no need to rush!! Soon it will all be over.

ME: Hooray! back to Civvy Street.

ADOLPH: Civvy Street is no more! It was destroyed by zer bombs of mine Luftwaffe.

We were pressing on down the dusty road towards Souk Arras a hundred miles from the front. At Oued Athmenia, we got into a secondary road. We were on a high plateau, the sun overhead, the endless jolting finally made you numb. At the next break Driver Shepherd took over. Budden emerged from behind a tree, shaking off the drips. 'Right Milligan, off we go.'

'I'm not Milligan sir,' said Shepherd, in a hurt voice.

'Oh it's *you* Shepherd, good!'

Voice from back of truck. 'It's the Good Shepherd sir.'

19 Battery was now to part from the main body of the Regiment. *They* went to spend the night at Guelma (the dirty swines) while *we*, the lilywhite boys, went on half the distance again, into a night bivouac outside Souk Arras.

Meantime at No. 10 Downing Street.

Churchill in bed sipping brandy. Enter Alanbrook.

LORD ALANBROOK: Prime Min. have you seen the bill for Singapore?

HON. W. CHURCHILL: I know – those Japa-bloody-knees – why couldn't they come round the front?

LORD ALANBROOK: They're Tradesmen. Any news of Randolph?

HON. W. CHURCHILL: He's out in Yugoslavia with that Piss-Artist Evelyn Waugh.

Now read on:

15 Feb. en route to Le Kef. Souk Arras lay along the head waters of the Mejerda River which later swept down and watered the vineyards of the great Mejerda Valley. Thought you'd like to know. Everywhere this dusty light sand coloured soil reflected the sun's glare so we used our anti-gas goggles. Everywhere seemed parched, and on this the fourth day of driving, our faces were sore. The horse flies! These buggers would break the skin and suck your blood, given 2 minutes they could give you anaemia. You had to hit them the *moment* they landed, a split second later was too late. Men with slow reflexes suffered, like Forrest, who was covered in bites and great bruises where he had hit at them and missed. The more he missed, the harder he hit. 'I wish I was Jordy Liddel,' he moaned. 'When they bite him, they fall off dead.'

'It's all that shit he works with.'

About 12.15 Mr Budden said 'Milligan, we have just crossed the border into Tunisia.'

'I'll carve a statue at once.'

On the border was Sakiet Sidi Youseff, where there was some kind of mine. A few donkeys and Arabs were at a pit head or shaft out of which ran a narrow rail, from inside the hole a tipper truck would appear with the powder produce which they shovelled into sacks on the donkeys.

'Where did you spend your last holidays Milligan,' Mr Budden broke in.

'I went with some friends to Whitesand Bay in Cornwall.'

'. . . Cornwall? Cornwall.' He put his binoculars up.

'You can't see it from here sir.'

'I'm not *looking* for Cornwall.'

The journey had covered us all in fine white powdery dust giving us the appearance of old men. Sid Price started to walk bent double like an old Yokel, within seconds the whole battery were doing it, Africa rang to the sound of 'Oh Arrrr! Oi be seventy three oi be in Zummerzet.' At the head of the column Major Chater Jack sat watching us. 'It's going to be a long hard war,' he was saying. I can still see his amused smile, especially as Woods, his batman, *was* from Somerset.

'Lot o' daft idiots zur,' he said to the Major.

'Yes Woods, a lot of daft idiots, but I fear you and I are stuck with 'em. The thing to do is keep them well camouflaged.' We were off again, and owing to a laundry crisis I was living dangerously, no underwear!

15 Feb. 1200 hours. 'Le Kef 20 Kilometers.' The road started to climb at an alarming angle, hairpin bend after hairpin bend we laboured, finally the engines started to boil and Chater Jack called a halt. We were in a defile. The dramatic landscape looked like Daumier's drawings for The Divine Comedy. The rocks around abounded with lizards, to my delight a chameleon was rainbowing around a tree, Shepherd was amazed at the colour changes. 'How in God's name can they do that,' he said. 'It's clean living,' I said. 'If you stopped playing with yourself you could do it.' Looking along the line one caught sight of the odd Gunner piddling against the wheels. I don't understand it! They have to clean their own transport, and then, when they've got the whole of Africa, they piss on their own lorries!

Valentine Dyall acting out World War II

The Battery Diary:

1500 hrs. Went into hide west of Le Kef.

(Cowards!) 'What's Le Kef mean,' asked White. 'It means The Kef' I explained. I watched some ants moving a dead grasshopper – 'What you doing?' says Edgington with a tea mug welded to his right hand.

'Watching ants.'

'I wonder what killed him,' said Edge, now squatting.

'It would be his heart.'

'We'll have to wait for the autopsy.'

'That might be too late, with his heart an autopsy could kill him.'

I angered a bull ant with a twig.

'Careful now,' says Edgington.

The bull ant was tugging at the twig.

'Don't let him get hold of it mate,' says Edge, 'or he'll beat the shit out of you.'

All eyes aloft. Two more squadrons of Boston Bombers appeared, the engines groaning under the weight of bombs. How clean it all looked up there. By sundown we were all pissed off doing nothing. Officers tried to occupy us with things like 'Do that top button up.' They were then hard put to it to think of something to do next, they settled for 'Undo that top button.'

'What's the time?' says Gunner Chalky White.

'You want to know the *time*?'

'I thought it would be exciting.'

'All right,' I said, 'it's 5.24.'

'Can I hear it again?'

'I'm sorry it's gone – but I can let you have 5.25.'

'Oh no,' he shook his head sadly, 'I like the old times better.' I wrote a few letters. The one to Louise made me so hot I had to lie down in the shade. I tell you Bromide was useless!!!

MILLIGAN: Hellow Huston Control! descending for soft landing on Louise.

BASE: What's it look like?
MILLIGAN: Arrrgggh Knickers! Knockers!

'Char?' says Edgington handing me a mug of tea.

'You have interrupted my midday erotic fantasy!'

'Yes, I smelt burning hairs, and I was afeared for your trousers.' I sipped the tea. 'How's the journey in M Truck?'

'Bloody murder! Seats are wood, only trouble my arse isn't.'

'I miss not being able to play with the band,' I said.

'Me too,' he said, 'at least you can have a blow on yer bugle, me, where do you get a piano in lovely flyblown Le Kef?'

'Report sick, tell 'em you are suffering from Piano withdrawal.'

'He'll only give me one in tablet form.'

'Then it could open up the music world! And now! Franz Edgington, wearing a hedgehog skin loin cloth, will play Grieg's A Minor on an upright Tablet and scream.'

It was 5.20 p.m. At this time in civvy street I'd have been breaking my soul in the dull lit boredom at a wooden table in the Woolwich Arsenal Dockyard. Mr Rose the foreman would be saying 'You call *this* a day's work Milligan?' And I'd say 'Yes.' About now, they'd all be thinking of 5.30 and tucking their little thermos flasks in little cardboard briefcases and folding up the greaseproof paper for the morrow. Even if I got killed, it was better than that. Of course, if I got killed I might change my mind.

'Eggs again?' said Chalky White. 'We'll all be egg bound soon. There's no happy in between. Back at X Camp we all had the runs, now we're all bound up like bloody concrete.'

'True, I suppose the moment we get into action we'll all have the shits again,' I said.

'I wonder what it's like.'

'The shits?'

'No . . . action.'

'We'll soon know all about it.'

'They say it's very noisy.'

'Action?'
'No, the shits.'

It was night now – distant flashes of gunfire lit the sky.
Men sat in groups, talking, laughing, then, one by one,
crawled into the pit. In the dark, cigarette ends glowed like
fireflies. Somewhere, a long way off, a goat bleated, and a lot
of good it did him. While we slept the First Army was having
a bloody conflict establishing the character of the campaign.
In the mountains, there was no scope for dashing armoured
division pursuits on the flat as the Eighth Army had enjoyed.
This was an arduous vicious slogging match of small groups
of Infantry charging up hill tops at bayonet point. And on
this particular night all hell was being let loose in the Kasserine Pass with Rommel at his cavalier best destroying the
American opposition.

Battery Diary: 16 Feb. 1943

*. . . Battery Commander, and Gun Position Officer to El Aroussa
via Le Kef to report to C.R.A. 6th Armoured Div. Battery to move to
hide west of Gafour.*

'Why do they keep hidin' us,' says Chalky. 'I'm not
ashamed of being a Gunner.'

We bade farewell to lovely shit-laden Le Kef and set off in
our little Khaki Noddy Cars.

A sign 'Dust means death,' Shepherd commented. 'Aye, if
ye get too much in yer lungs it kills ye,' he says. We passed
camouflaged ammo dumps, rear Echelon vehicles, tents,
bivvys etc. Crossing the road ahead were what would seem
like bundles of rags on legs, carrying rifles and gas stoves.

'They're Goums,' said Lt Budden.

'Goons?' I giggled.

'GOUMIERS! French African Troops you illiterate
fellow.'

'Personally sir, I think it's the Irish Guards in drag.' The
Goums were accompanied by wives, children, chickens,
goats, dogs, and what looked like the entire contents of

Harrods furniture repository. The Goums were right. We should take our women to war, khaki knickers and all.

'Wake up darling.'

'What is it dear.'

'Those awful Germans want fighting dear.'

'Not again. I killed three yesterday.'

'Here's your sandwiches and rifle. Try and not use the bayonet dear, you know what a mess it makes on the carpet.' We were being waved across by a Military Policeman. His trousers had knife-edge creases, even his legs had knife-edge creases. His webbing was blinding white, his brass-work flashed in the sun like gold bayonets. He saluted Lt Budden. 'Try and go slow, sir, we've had three straffings this morning, it's the dust.'

'You must get a Hoover,' I said to him, and drove on.

'*That*, Milligan,' said Budden, 'was what I call *real* bull-shit.'

'Ah! So you *can* tell the difference sir.'

I told him an idea to end the war. All you do is drop fifty English char ladies on the Führer's bunker. In one week the Hun would be broken. 'Come on now, I'm not 'avin' all those men in jack boots stompin' on my polished floor. Never mind about silly old Stalingrad, you sit down and I'll bring you a nice cup of tea and a cheese roll for Mr Goering.'

We passed Gafour, another dung village, and pulled up on a flat rocky plateau with stunted trees and scrub, but no Porridge.

'Listen sir,' I said, 'gunfire!'

'Yes,' said Lt Budden, 'there's a lot of it about.'

A mile to our left towered the blue grey shape of Djbel Eich Cheid, rising some thousand metres. Moving towards us in a cloud of dust was a flock of goats attended by a small boy, whose sole occupation was to hit them and shout 'Yeaeah'. Growing almost in secrecy were cornflowers. This little flower was the first to bloom in Hiroshima after the holocaust; so much for the power of the Atom. Lurching hither, his hat on sideways was the Great Edgington. He carried yet *another* mug of tea. How *did* he manage to brew up so quick? 'I'll tell you,' he said. 'It's fear.'

Hitlergram No. 1560934a

FÜHRER: Tea – zat is how ve will break zer Britisher!

MESSERSCHMIDT: A great idea mein Führer.

FÜHRER: Zer Englanders, zey like make drink tea? – zis is vat I vant you should make, you vill build eine Tank – zis Tank vill inside a bladder have – in zer bladder ve have zer smell of zer NAAFI tea – we sneak zer tank up on zer Tommy Lines, at 4 o'clocken, zer gun barrel, we squirt zer NAAFI tea smell up zere trouser legs.

MESSERSCHMIDT: Squirt ze tea Schmell?

HITLER: Zen zer Tommy will jump up and run vid zer mug tovords zer tea-schmell-tank. Zen we shoot-bang-fire!

MESS: Zis vill finish zer Englanders.

We listened to the BBC one o'clock news. Stewart Hibberd was telling us the First Army troops had 'successfully disengaged the enemy,' this meant we'd taken a bashing. Why not 'British troops confuse enemy by refusing to fight.'

The little shepherd boy stood watching with eyes like huge brown liquid marbles. 'Quelle est votre nom?' I asked.

'Mahomet,' he said.

'Me Spike Milligan,' I said.

I gave him some boiled sweets, it came as a shock when I realised he wasn't quite sure what they were, I had to eat one to show him. We take a lot of things for granted. The afternoon was warm. Some lads, shirts off, basking in the sun, white bodies, eyes closed, what were they thinking? Pint at the Pub? Watching Millwall at the Den? A walk with the Girl on Sunday? See? The lazy sods, that's all they ever think of! Booze, Football and Sex.

The afternoon was passing very slowly, we threw stones, broke branches off trees, played Pontoon, we played stones, broke Pontoon and threw trees. We walked around. We sat down. We stood up. We smoked. 'Christ if only we had an air raid or measles.' Spike Deans had bought two chickens off an Arab, and for three francs each we could partake of them for din-din! That night we sat dining on roast chicken and drinking the last bottle of wine. We drank and sang 'I'll be seeing you in all the old familiar places'. In the distance we could hear guns. In the shadows our own guns stood silent in their covers. Soon it would be their turn.

17th Feb. Dawn. Yawning, I slipped the Humber into gear. 'Rendezvous Map Reference 68039' said Lt Budden. 'You holidayed in Cornwall you say?'

The road was difficult. Come to think of it, so was I. It was marked camel track and it took us to El Aroussa, a small wayside railway station, now a smoking ruin. Around it were the blackened skeletons of a dozen or so lorries. Inside shattered buildings were blood spattered walls, blood soaked battle dress jackets and trousers. An old Arab, all that was left of the station staff ('Toute morte') described how it happened. Stukas had come yesterday, in a few minutes it was all over.

'Christ,' says Bdr Sherwood. 'What's happened?'

'Don't worry, these are only the cheap seats,' I said.

'He must have been a bad driver,' said Chalky White. The humour was a bit forced. None of us were sure what to say. The officers were grouped around a map, and appeared more excited than is good for English gentlemen.

'What are they on?' said Chalky.

'Vitamin B' I said.

Up the line comes Chater Jack's truck. 'Prepare to move! Lads, Yoiks, Tally Ho!'

We followed him towards Bou Arada. Half a mile on he turned left across the railway lines, down a bank, over a dusty wheat field towards a small farm nestling at the foot of the Djbel Rihane (nicknamed 'Grandstand Hill'). Behind, the great khaki guns rolled like fat babies as they negotiated the bosomy terrain. The silence was broken by the sharp crack of artillery.

'They sound like Mediums,' said Lt Budden.

'Too small sir,' I said. 'I take Outsize.'

Sergeant Dawson raced past on his motorbike; when we arrived at the farm, he was waiting with the Major, soon the area was a mass of frenetic action.

'Scrim Nets on!'

'Disperse Wireless Trucks under those trees!'

'Monkey trucks prepare to lay ten-mile telephone line!'

'All guns in that Wadi there!'

'Bombardier? Form OP Party!'

'For God's sake,' I said, 'There's more orders than men.' Edgington joined in, 'All Gunners stand on one leg and lean eastward.'

The guns were towed into a Wadi. Command Post tent appeared to have been put up by trainee Wolf Cubs. Bren guns were mounted against aircraft. 'Lucky sods,' said White, 'all they got to do is scratch their balls and look up.'

The 200 lb mustard coloured shells were being unloaded and stacked. Signallers were lugging communications equip-

19 Battery gunners specially marked with large white crosses to make them easier targets for the Germans

ment into the Command Post, specialists were putting up Artillery Boards and all those fiddling instruments that computed which German the shell would hit. Of course they could have put all the names in a hat. A trestle table was erected for the Tannoy Control. Next to it were the telephone and the wireless set. Cables were run to the gun positions, loudspeakers at each sub-section connected and tested. It worked like this. Place loudspeaker near gun, connect wire from Command Post, press button on top of loudspeaker at Gun Position. Immediately light flashes in Command Post control panel.

'Hello B Sub. You're flashing, can you hear me?'

'Yes, but we're not B Sub, we're A Sub.'

'Oh fuck, can you flash again?'

'I'm not going to become a flasher fer anybody.'

Signallers are laying a line to the Waggon Lines, the place for vital supplies, vehicles, cowards, and Porridge. It is important to appear busy. Gunner White was cunningly going round with an empty DDT tin, when questioned, he would spring to attention and say 'Delousing Sah!' and he got away with it. On the next page I have drawn from diary a plan of the 19 Battery layout including the sleeping accommodation.

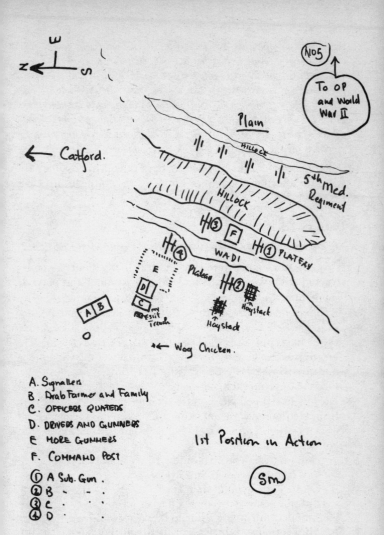

A. Signallers
B. Arab Farmer and Family
C. OFFICERS QUARTERS
D. DRIVERS AND GUNNERS
E. MORE GUNNERS
F. COMMAND POST

① A Sub. Gun .
② B . " .
③ C " .
④ D " .

1st Position in Action

Sm

Major Chater Jack's letter of the time recounts:

'... *perhaps an idea of what my H.Q. looks like would be possible,*

69

but to get the atmosphere is impossible. It is rather like one of the original structures at K.K.* but there is very much more of it. Tony (Goldsmith) and I have bedding at one end handy to us, our wireless, telephone and loudspeaker systems to the guns. In the middle is a table, some charts and an electric light run by bringing in the headlight of the vehicle outside. At the other end is Wood (Batman) and a few others who are this moment trying to get a primus stove going for tea, since we have just had 'stand down' as the sun rises . . .'

Ridiculous! *Sit* down yes, but *stand* down, impossible! It was late afternoon, we were hurrying to establish an O.P. before dark.

Battery Diary:

19 Battery moved into action, north of Bou Arada. Map Ref. 6006.

By nightfall guns were dug in, and living quarters constructed. In my mud hut I took out my trumpet and played 'Lili Marlene'.

* I never found out what this meant.

A 7·2 Howitzer being made ready for its first time in action – Bou Arada Feb. 1943

Nazi News Flash

ROMMEL: Hear zat? Zis man *must* be captured, he has shown considerable initiative! To play a German tune *behind* zer Allied Lines, he must have zer complete confidence of General von Alexander. We must capture zis Golden Englander Trumpet-speiler!

VON HATATIME: How can ve use him?

ROMMEL: First we make him Field Marshall Spike von Milligan and Company Limited Nazi Holdings, Bankers Hill Samuels then he will face the Allied Line and play 'Charge!' Ven zer British are almost up to our lines he will play 'Retreat', they will withdraw, zen he will play 'Charge' again, zen 'Retreat'. After five hours zer Britishers vill be, how you say?

VON H: Shagged out!

ROMMEL: Ya. Shagged out!

VON H: Supposing he refuses?

ROMMEL: He von't I have zomething here, he will do anything for!
Here Rommel hands Von Hatatime a photograph. Von H. looks, has seventeen premature ejaculations, staggers, backs forwards, sideways, sweat pouring from his Field Marshall's baton, speaks.

VON H: Mein Gott. Louise from Bexhill!

ROMMEL: Look at zose Knockers.

VON H: Vunderschoen! Now I know why zey call you zer Foxtrot of the Desert.

The Signallers were all inside the Arab hut which now glowed yellow with improvised oil lamps. I checked my Tommy gun for the night. I had continually worked out in my mind the precautions I would take if confronted by Germans. It was a simple but highly effective plan, I would raise my hands above my head and say 'I surrender.'

Through our door came Sergeant Dawson! Grinning evilly he removed the blankets from my weary body.

'We're looking for our first hero casualty. We're laying a line to the O.P.'

'Tonight?'

'Yes.'

'I was just going to bed, it's Rita Hayworth's turn.'

'Get yer bloody boots on.'

'I must get my rest Sarge – people are saying I'm finished.'

'I'll tell you when you'll be finished. Four o'clock tomorrow morning.'

I pulled my boots on, got my pliers, Tommy gun, and slid into the dark. The detail was, L/Bdr Sherwoods and his Bren Carrier, Sgt Dawson, Gunners Hart, Webster, Milligan and Bdr Fuller, who knew where the O.P. was. Dawson told us 'Silence is imperative.' We set off being imperatively silent which couldn't be heard because of the noise of the Bren Carrier. We walked behind with a cable drum that went clinkety-clank. Why? The 'hole' in the cable drum was *square* but the spindle was round. We all spoke in hysterical whispers. God knows why, to communicate we had to shout above the engine. As this charade went on, we started to giggle, then outright laughter. 'Stop the bloody Bren' shouted Dawson, himself on the verge of laughter. There was a suppressed silence. Unable to stand it, we all burst out laughing again.

'Stop it at once!' said Dawson through his own laughter. We stopped. 'Now stop it, or I'll kill the bloody lot of you.' A white star shell lit the night.

'What's that?' said Ernie Hart.

'That, Ernie, means that a child has been born in Bethlehem,' I said.

'Well, he's two months late and the wrong bloody map reference.' Another two star shells.

'She's had triplets,' said Ernie. After an hour we reached the O.P. hill.

'This way,' said Bombardier Fuller. Birch and I followed with reel.

'Stop that fokin' noise,' hissed an angry Irish voice, 'you'll get us all fokin' mortared.'

We took the spindle from the drum and unwound by hand. More flares, suddenly a rapid burst of automatic fire. It was a Spandau, a return burst, the unmistakable chug, chug, chug of a Bren gun. A flare silhouetted us beautifully for the whole Afrika Korps to see. 'Freeze,' hissed Fuller. I had one leg raised when he said it. Somewhere a German O.P. officer was saying 'Himmel! zey are using one-legged soldiers.' The flares fade. Fuller says 'I'm lost.'

'I thought you'd never say it,' I said.

We groped our way back to the party who were inside the Bren practising fear and smoking. Dawson attached a phone to the line.

'Hello, Gun Position here.'

'This is Sergeant Dawson. Tell Major Chater Jack we can't find the bloody O.P., will it be all right tomorrow?' We waited. 'Yes' Chater said 'OK tomorrow, but before first light.' 'Let's bugger off,' said Dawson.

We piled into the carrier. I looked up. What a sky! The heavens encrusted with stars, the milky way hung like a luminous veil across the firmament.

'Halt.' Two sentries loomed in the dark. 'Friend or Foe?'

'Friends,' we all screamed from the grovelling position.

'What's the password?'

Dawson tried explaining in a thick Jordy accent, 'Why mon, we doant noe. Weaire Gooners from 56 Artilury, weaire layin a lyine.' The accent was sufficient for us to pass. About one o'clock we arrived at the G.P. Our guns were firing. What a bloody noise. What in heaven's name did they think they were doing – it was past midnight! What would the neighbours say? Soldiers needed rest. They have to get up every morning looking lovely for their Regiments.

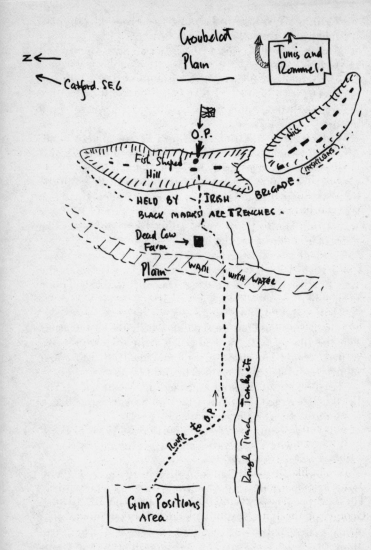

Map of Route to O.P.

GENERAL MONTGOMERY: Have you seen Gunner Milligan this morning?

GENERAL ALEXANDER: No, why?

GENERAL MONTGOMERY: He looks so tired and washed out. The Germans shouldn't really see him like that.

GENERAL ALEXANDER: By Jove yes, I'll ask him to see the M.O.

Later at the M.O.:

GNR MILLIGAN: I don't know, every morning I wake up listless and jaded and the men are talking.

M.O.: Milligan, you're suffering from night-starvation. I want you to wake up five times a night and drink three gallons of Porridge.

Next morning:

GENERAL MONTGOMERY: Seen Milligan this morning?

GENERAL ALEXANDER: Yes, he's back to his old self, thanks to

TOGETHER: Porridge!

I got to bed. Yawning, I pulled the blankets over me, doused the lamp and slid into dreamlit hours of dark freedom. To sleep under the ear shattering blasts of our guns seemed impossible, yet as they thundered in the night towards Medjez el Bab, we slept like babes. It seemed I had just put my lovely head to pillow when the boot of the sentry delicately kicked me conscious.

'Milligan.'

'Mmmm? Arggggg Schmatter Gwanpizorf.'

'You and Fuller have got to connect the O.P. line.'

'Whassermarrer? Ahhhhhhhbalztoyer alllll.'

'There's early breakfast laid on for you.'

'I don't like people laying on my food!'

It was 05.00 hours, it wasn't fair! Who invented early? The late people were much happier, like the Late King George, or the Late Rasputin. I didn't bother to wash or shave. Red-eyed I ambled to the Cook House. 'How long you been dead?' said the Cook. The morning air was cool, light blue mist cast a hazy veil over the landscape. The dawn peace was shattered by the Fifth Mediums laying down a barrage. Breakfast was a surprise. The new Compo K rations had arrived, cases of tinned and dehydrated foods. We had scrambled egg, sausages and Ahhha Porridge.

'They're just fattening you up for the kill,' said the Cook.

o6oo: Bombardier Fuller and I set off. We skirted our guns to avoid the muzzle blast and Porridge. The ground was covered with a very light dew that was now drying out. Every twenty yards we stapled the wire to the ground.

The 1st round in anger – 19 Battery at War

The sun came up, it was going to be a lovely day. Reaching the foot of the hill Bdr Fuller suddenly 'remembered' where the O.P. was, 'We was too far to the left.' (We?) 'You (You?) go and bring it this way.' I walked to where we'd dumped the cable. Unbeknown, I was under enemy observation. WHOOSH-BANG! Behind me a purple and red explosion. I was so surprised I walked to where it had happened when WHOSSH-BAM another one; I didn't like it, dropping the cable drum I made a tactical withdrawal to the foot of the hill.

'They must have seen you,' says Fuller, a master of the

*British Troops
cutting German
Laundry Lines*

obvious. Two more burst behind the crest, half a dozen more, they were searching for us. Then all quiet.

'Look,' I said, 'this is bloody dangerous work. I'm going to put in for a rise.'

'I (I?) must get this bloody line finished,' says Fuller, 'O.P. is straight up to the right of that tree.'

I payed out the line as he went forward. Nearer the crest he started to crouch and finally disappeared into the scrub. Now and then I'd feel a tug on the line as he freed it from some obstruction. I was holding the line when two Bren carriers of infantry passed down the hill to my right.

'Fishing, mate?' said a laconic voice. I made a time honoured gesture. Fuller re-emerged.

'Everything OK?' I asked.

'Yes.'

'Who's up there?'

'Lt Goldsmith and Bdr Edwards.'

'Let's get back,' I said. I now produced my new pipe, which I had bought to try and avoid smoking those bloody awful V's. Having a pipe clenched in your teeth seemed to make you feel calm, thoughtful, unflappable.

Major Chater Jack: I see Milligan is smoking a pipe.
Sgt Dawson: Yes sir.
Major Chater Jack: He looks very good smoking it.
Sgt Dawson: Yes sir.
Major Chater Jack: He looks manly.
Sgt Dawson: Very manly.
Major Chater Jack: Unflappable?
Sgt Dawson: Definitely unflappable!
Major Chater Jack: What's he like as a soldier?
Sgt Dawson: Bloody awful sir.

Rather than go back to the gun position we hung around at the foot of the O.P. hill yarning and smoking. Finally, towards evening, we started back.

'It was all a bit of an anti-climax,' Fuller said.

'Yes. I wonder which bit it was?'

I felt my chin. I had a three day growth. A dust storm was starting to blow up, I couldn't decide whether it was German or one of ours. In the middle of it, a staff car emerged from across the fields.

Me: Look Frank! In the middle of it, a staff car has emerged from across the fields!

It was General Alexander with some staff officers. They got out, pointed in all directions, leaped back in the car and shot off at speed. The rich have all the fun! Dusty and tired we arrived at the gun position. Lt Joe Mostyn had just returned from a meal with an Arab sheik. 'I had to eat three bloody sheeps' eyes!'

'Really?' I said, 'Bend down and you should be able to see out the back.'

Poor old Joe! He was not particularly good at Gunnery! On his first day at an O.P. he scored ten direct hits, – on a field. I pointed out there were no Germans in it.

'Ah,' he said, 'they may fall in the holes.'

'Of course,' I said, 'German Division surrenders with twisted ankle.'

'You've *got* to miss sometimes,' he said, 'it's good for business! What a war! There I was just doing well in the Schmutter Trade, and this Schmoch Hitler comes along so, I have to switch from outsize blouses to battle-dresses. I'm just starting to do well again when *I* get called up. *Me* a soldier? This major says "Mostyn, with your head for figures you're ideal for the R.A." So here I am wasting shells, *ten* shells, that's see ... nearly £400 quid, *wasted*, for that I could have made three hundred and ten battle-dresses.'

The I.G. at war

I'm Captain Blenkinsop, I.G.,
Sent by mistake across the sea,
To land upon this dismal shore
And find myself involved in war.
Sad is the tale I have to tell –
For a man like me this war is hell.
For how can anyone expect,
My fall of shot to prove correct,
When everything I tell the guns,
Is interfered with by the Huns?
When bombs are dropping down in rows
How can I make my traverse close.
Or take a bearing on the Pole
While cowering in a muddy hole?
It's plain that the opposing forces,
Have not been on the proper courses.
But, worst of all, the other day,
When I was checking someone's lay,
The Germans rushed the gun position
Without the Commandant's permission.
I had to meet them, man to man,
Armed only with a Tetley fan.
O send me back to Salisbury Plain
And never let me rove again!

Larkhill's the only place for me,
Where I could live at ease and free
And frame, with sharpened pencil stroke
A barrage of predicted smoke.
Worked out for sixteen different breezes,
With extra graphs, in case it freezes,
For non-rigidity corrected,
And on a Merton Grid projected!
O take me to the R.A. Mess,
To dwell in red brick happiness,
Enfold my body, leather chair,
And let me fight the War from there!

Lt Tony Goldsmith

18.20 hours. I retired to our mud hut, threw myself on my bed. My second day in action and not killed yet! By God the Germans were bad shots! Next door to us were the Arab farmer, his wife and two kids, a boy of six and a girl about four. I knew they must be having a rough time so I occasionally took them a tin of steak and kidney pudding. What words of comfort did the Arab mother have for her children? How did she explain away the thunder of our guns, what did she say we were? Good? Bad? I suppose the little Arab boy is a man now and works the same land, perhaps he's getting a

A direct hit on a German Laundry

better life. I wonder if he remembers the gunner who made a rabbit's head from a handkerchief and made it wiggle its ears. He might be telling his children 'So this silly bugger comes up, ties a few knots in his handkerchief and I was supposed to laugh. Silly sod!' The oil lamps cast a yellow glow, shadows wavered on faces in the playing light. The guns, silent for the past hour, started a Harassing Fire Task. Somewhere, some German was about to receive 200 pounds of exploding iron.

Harassing Fire had no rhythm . . . That was the idea . . . you fired at aggravating intervals. It was the Chinese water torture with solids.

Ernie Hart: What was it like at the O.P.?
Me: Nothing much I was shelled a bit.
Ernie: What *real* shells?
Me: Oh no, just imitations.
Ernie: Were they near?
Me: Pretty near. They fell in the same country.
Hart: We had to take a line to the top of Djbel Rihane, near the Mosque.
Me: Mosque?
Hart: Yes, it was a ruin.
Me: Shows you what drink can do.
Hart: We could see Jerry from the top.
Me: Anybody we knew?
Hart: We could even see 'em queueing up for grub.
A Voice: What's the time?
Me: It's nearly eleven.
Hart: Feels like two in the morning.
Me: You must be feeling the wrong part.

He pulled the blankets up and moved down into his pit.

Me: Just think, if Gladstone was alive today he'd be a hundred and fifty-seven. Men cannot live by bread alone!
Hart: Wot you talkin' about? Go to sleep for Christ sake.
Me: Very well, but if Gladstone comes through that door and asks for a slice of bread alone, don't say I didn't warn you!

At this, Gunner Milligan rolled on his side, closed his eyes and dreamed he was fronting a twenty-four piece orchestra. They all wore black jackets but *He* was wearing a *white* one, playing great trumpet solos that had people crowding the stand. Lily was there and he ignored her, at which moment Rita Hayworth called for him in a Rolls Royce that she drove right up to the bandstand. He screws Hayworth in the back of the Rolls, then takes another chorus on the trumpet.

Dawn 20th Feb. 1943. A khaki creature was shaking me. 'Come on Harry James stand to . . .' 'Stand Two? I can't stand one.'

It was 0400 hours. 0400 hours? There was no such time, it had been invented by Hitler to break us. I staggered out into the chill morning darkness. Bombardier Edwards posted me in a trench directly outside the officers' hut.

'Get in, keep your eyes open, stay in that hole. If you get killed, just lay down and we'll fill it in.'

'Very funny,' I said to him. 'With your sense of humour you should be on the other side.'

I was alone in the hole in the ground in Africa. It was very quiet. All the guns had stopped firing. They usually did in the small hours, even wars get tired. There was the distant yapping of Arab farm dogs. I wondered when the bloody animals ever slept. As eyes focused to the dark I could see the black shapes that were the block outlines of the huts, the Bren carrier, the wireless trucks, the tracery of the scrim nets. Above, the heavens with stars glittering in the traverse of the sky. The officers' hut door opened, I saw the outline of Major Chater Jack followed by Goldsmith. Seeing the top half of a human in a hole he said 'My God, who's that?'

'Gunner Milligan sir.'

'What's the matter? I thought you were taller!'

'I'm in a hole sir.'

I heard Chater Jack chuckle. He said something to Goldsmith and they both returned convulsed with suppressed laughter.

I was again alone in a hole in Africa. At this moment among the warring nations there were literally hundreds of thousands of little men, all standing in holes, in France,

Germany, Poland, Russia. What a lot of bloody fools we must look! The door of the officers' hut opened again. The mountainous figure of Chater Jack's batman, Woods, loomed towards me. He handed me a cup of tea 'With the Boss's compliments,' he said. I sipped the tea – there must be some mistake! It had *whisky* in!! I'd better hurry. I gulped it down and as I finished Gunner Woods returned. 'Were there whisky in thart tea?' he said. I nodded.

'Well bugger oi down dead,' he said, 'that were Major's tea.'

Woods had approached me with the mind of a boy of twelve and left with one of thirteen. Experience ages a man. The first light was quickening the morning sky. Ghostly outlines were gradually turning into detailed reality as the covers of night fell off, we were all thinking, breakfast! Loudspeakers crackled into life. 'Take Post!' Gunners dropped their food and ran to the guns, to cries of 'Fuck our luck.' I discovered that some swine had stolen my shaving brush, so I stole someone else's. I had an early breakfast, and was de-

Winners of the 1st Army Trilby Hat Contest

83

tailed to check the O.P. line. I liked going. It took me away from the mob and gave me a sense of freedom. I told Shapiro I wanted him to come with me.

'Oh no,' he said, 'I can't come, my tin hat doesn't fit properly.'.

'You're a hat cutter, it's your own bloody fault.'

'OK,' he grinned.

Battery Diary: 20 Feb. 1943

Activity of enemy patrols in the hills west of Battery has increased considerably. 6 Commandoes have come up on Division Front. Degree of alertness increased to one third stand to during hours of darkness. Bombing and listening posts established in gully running north into hills. 936338 W/Bdr Jones L. W. accidentally wounded during action exercise.

Shapiro and I trudged dustily along the line.

'Some bastard's stole my shaving brush,' I said.

'That's funny, some bastard's stolen mine.'

We were walking over wheat fields now flattened by war machines. It was magnificent country, spring was at hand, the wild flowers were beginning to sprout, the wheat crops were about a foot high, and lush broad beans were about to flower. Compared with the English variety, these were giants, and there were acres and acres of them around El Aroussa flat lands. This was rich and fertile growing country, but depended on rain, the ancient Roman irrigation system having fallen into ruin. Another plant, Borage, was growing freely in the ditches as were little blue and red anemones that grew among the wheat stalks. Broom was about to bud. Looking back towards the guns, we were in a broad flat valley with high hills and mountains to our right, some craggy and precipitous, some smooth and rolling like the South Downs. Among the flat rock faces, lizards, chameleons and an occasional gecko would be found taking the warmth of the rocks. A few white cabbage butterflies had appeared along with several orange tips. In the evenings swifts appeared, from where I'll never know. The African sky was like most other skies, save it had the quality of brilliant light. One felt oneself being urged to paint, paint, paint! As we trudged forward I wrote on various stones little messages for those who might follow in our footsteps.

'This way for World War II,' or 'Hello Soldier, having fun.'

'You have just passed Go. Collect 200 pounds.'

'Insure *now* with the Prudential.'

Shapiro was patting his pockets . . . 'Got a fag?'

Me: Yes.

Shapiro: Since we have been in action I've smoked more.

Me: I've got plenty since I smoked a pipe.

Shapiro: Ta.

I lit him up and then lit my pipe.

Shapiro: What's it like with a pipe?

'It's a psychological difference.'

'What's that mean?'

'I don't know. I read it in a medical book.'

'Let me try!'

He took the pipe, drew, inhaled, then burst out coughing. His eyes started to water,

'Ohhh dear! Fucking terrible! How do you inhale that crap?'

'You don't.'

'Now he tells me. I'll stick to fags.'

'Yes, stick to yours.'

Shapiro: Tell you what, you want to sell me some?

Me: You come quickly on the hour!

Shapiro: How much?

Me: How much you got?

Shapiro: You thieving sod.

Me: It's twenty fags, twenty francs. Business is business. We are fighting a capitalist war, so it's twenty francs!

Shapiro unbuttons his left hand battle-dress pocket. You would tell by the wear and tear on the leading edges it was where he kept his lolly. He took out his pay book, opened it, laying between the leaves was 500 francs.

'You done a robbery?' I said.

'No, I save it and send it home to my mother, and she buys houses with it.'

Gunner Milligan selling cigarettes to Gunner Shapiro in the heat of battle

He counted me out two tens.

'You're a bloody robber,' he said smiling. I could but think of the added burden he had being Jewish. If the Germans took him prisoner . . .

The line tested, we made for the Bren Carrier at the bottom of the hill. 'Anybody in?' I called. Bombardier Sherwood appeared from under the scrim net. 'Ahh! you're *just* in time for tea.' Bombardier Hart was in the very act of pouring it. He looked up.

'Cor, Cohen and Kelly! you don't half time it right.'

'We persecuted minorities have to use our nut.'

I untied my tea mug from my waist. 'Weee Craskkhhhh.' An eighty-eight! Then another and another and another, then lots of anothers – in all about twenty rounds. We hugged the side of the Bren Carrier. The smell of cordite drifted across, fragments of metal scattered around us. It stopped as suddenly as it started.

'I think Jerry can see the bloody lot of us *all* the time,' I said, 'whenever I've come up here, he's thrown a few over.'

'It's *you*, Milligan,' said Sherwood. 'You're a Jonah, get in the Bren Carrier and we'll throw you over the side.'

We drank our tea. After two days in action I knew the most dangerous gun in Africa was the 88 mm, its low trajectory gave no warning of approach.

'Who's at the O.P.' I asked.

'Tony Goldsmith and Spike Deans.'

'Have they had any tea?' I said.

'No,' said Sherwood.

'Fill my water bottle and I'll take some up.'

Carefully Sherwood filled it. I fixed it to my belt and started up the hill. I took no chances and kept to the right, as I neared the crest, I lay down and crawled.

'Where are you 19 Bty?' I coo-ed.

'This way,' said Spike Deans. 'We're the good-looking ones.'

They guided me by 'talking me down.' The view from the O.P. was magnificent. Below lay the vast Goubelat Plain, to our right, about five miles on, were two magnificent adjoining rocky peaks that rose sheer 500 feet above the plain, Garra el Kibira and Garra el Hamada, christened 'Queen Sheba's Tits'. At the foot lay El Kourzia, a great salt lagoon two to three miles in circumference. Around the main lagoon were dotted smaller lagoons and around the fringe, what appeared to be a pink scum. In fact it was hundreds of flamingoes. This vision, the name of Sheba, the sun, the crystal white and silver shimmer of the salt lagoon made boyhood readings of Rider Haggard come alive. It was a sight I can never forget, so engraved was it that I was able to dash it down straight onto the typewriter after a gap of thirty years. Further right of the lagoon were marshes, at the edge of which was a burnt-out Panzer Mark III. 'That shows what a careless cigarette can do,' said Lt Goldsmith.

Tea finished, I started to crawl back.

'Thank mother for the rabbit, Milligan,' said Goldsmith.

Back at the Carrier they were playing pontoon. I arrived as Sherwood had lost his Bren Carrier on a five card trick.

'Want to play?' said Hart.

'OK.'

'He's got twenty francs,' Shapiro was quick to say.

The game reached an alarming level, I had bet my own mother and three francs on two picture cards. I made thirty francs on the day and, on paper, I still own Sherwoods fruit-shop in Reading.

'That's me finished,' said Sherwood. 'Who's got a fag?'

'Shapiro,' I said quickly – WHOOSHHHHHBANG! WHOSSSHBANG! . . . 88's! 'See?' I said, 'They know you're Jewish.' Ten more rounds.

'I'm not *that* bloody Jewish,' says Shapiro face down.

Next a round of marker smoke. It was a guide for a bombing raid – twelve Stukas roared down, the noise of their engines was incredible – like howling wolves; above them, circling, were ME 109s. The Stukas dropped their eggs on the London Irish, the noise was frightening, the earth shook as bombs exploded and the sky shook as the Bofors hammered away. When the last bomb had dropped the Gunners Shapiro and Milligan, Pontoon Players Extraordinary, shot out from under the camouflage net and ran heroically to a nullah. We sat gasping, looked at each other, and burst out laughing.

'We didn't say goodbye,' I said. We bent over the stream and splashed water over our faces.

Some of the London Irish had copped it, we saw three stretchers loaded on to a Bren and driven away. Hooking on our small arms we trudged back across the dusty plain. A motorcycle was coming towards us. It was a young para-trooper.

'You know where the London Irish are?' he asked

'Yes, so do the bloody Luftwaffe,' I pointed. 'They're spread along the rear slope of that hill.'

'Ta,' he said. 'What mob are you?'

'Gunners. You Paras?'

'Yes.'

'You were in the first lot out here?'

'Yer. What a scramble, they dropped us on Bone, and the

bloody Arabs were waiting to buy our 'chutes as we landed, we had to fight 'em to make 'em let go.' He laughed, revved the engine, and roared away.

'He might have been a German spy,' said Shapiro, who'd remained strangely silent during the conversation.

'Don't be bloody daft Shap, he was too scruffy to be a Kraut.'

'He asked questions didn't he? You told him what mob we were.'

'I didn't, all I said was we were gunners, not the name of the Regiment.'

'Oh.'

'You can take your finger off the trigger now.'

'I was just playing safe. He *could* have been a German.'

'OK it *was* a German, I never let on you were Jewish.'

'Oh thank you, thank you very much, that's big, you didn't tell him I was Jewish, what you want, a receipt for it or something?' When we got back the guns were firing.

'They're busy,' I shouted to Shapiro.

'It's pay day,' he said.

I sat on my bed enjoying the evening meal, steak and kidney pudding. This really was a good life if you didn't want to think more than ten minutes ahead. We got money, grub, clothes, transport, travel, everything bar women, and we could dream of them at night. Some just thought of one woman, I thought of as many as I could. I don't suppose they knew, but I had Deanna Durbin and Joan Blondell *every* night until the fall of Tunis, if I had a good dinner I used to include Mae West. Other lads were smoking, fiddling with kit, sewing buttons, chatting or talking to the wall. I closed my eyes. It was time I had some letters! Wonder what Lily was doing. I knew what Louise would be doing! AHHHHHHHHHHRGGGG! Louise was the girl with big boobs and buttocks that had serviced me twice a week. Ahrggg!!! Someone was shaking me – it was me. No, someone else was shaking me! It was *him*!

The sentry, 'Stand to.'

Four o'clock already? Somewhere someone was removing the hours between sunset and sunrise, that or they were bringing four in the morning forward to eight at night. It was chilly. Silent. Again, I stood in a hole in the ground. Let me

On duty on a hole in the Ground for my King and Country

see first I'd face east for a few minutes, then I faced nor' nor' east, then south west and due west, next I sat on the edge of the hole and faced north. I then stood and revolved slowly round in a complete 360° circle, that is, I covered every known compass point in the world and all from a hole in the ground. Brilliant. I thought of a bar of soap. I unclipped the magazine of my Tommy gun. I said Hello to it. I clipped it back on again. I felt in my trouser pockets, I removed the contents, a broken comb, a pencil stub. I said Goodbye to them. I drew Ravel's Haunted Ballroom in the air. Next, I pulled the pockets inside out and shook the dust out. I whistled Van Gogh's Sunflower. I drew an imaginary line on my teeth. Now what? Don't just stand there – be creative! I reversed my tin hat, and stuck one finger in my ear. I felt up the sleeves of my battle-dress and pulled the sleeves of my pullover down over my wrists. I counted my nose, I listened for Germans. Silence, but who was making it? On an impulse I said 'Fish.'

A sentry loomed into sight. 'Spike?'

'Yes, who is it?'

'Ben Wenham.'

'We can still be friends.'

'What's the time?'

'04.20 hours. Mind you it's only a cheap watch, by an expensive one it would be at least 05.30.'

All quiet. I faced east. Yes, I'd stay facing east, that's where the sun would appear. The sun was rising *behind* me. I must be facing west, or was it because I had my tin hat on back to front, yes, that's it, I was facing east, but my hat wasn't, and all in a hole in the ground. 06.00 Stand Down. Thank God. Another two minutes and I'd have been certified. I took breakfast, clobbered Jock Webster and Shapiro. 'Sergeant Dawson says we're to go to the O.P. because we're not Protestants.'

My Diary: 23 Feb. 1943

Up at dawn. To O.P. with Shapiro and Webster. Shapiro reports someone has stolen his shaving-brush. This is the 5th day he's reported it. Anything rather than buy one. This will be my fifth continuous day as O.P. linesman. Arrived midday. Shelled . . .

The blast threw me to the ground. Webster and Shapiro doubled for cover, like idiots we ran *up* the hill, and jumped into a trench. Help! A mortar pit knee-deep in mortar bombs! Sitting quietly in the corner smoking a pipe was an old Irish Sergeant. I tapped Shapiro.

'Ask him if he wants to sell his fags.'

Several more shells fell around us. Christ! if one landed in this pit! . . . .

'Let's get out when it stops,' said Shapiro.

'Oh, youse will be safe in here lads,' said the Sergeant.

'Safe? In a pit full of bombs? Only the Irish . . .'

It went quiet. 'Right! *now!*' I said. 'Not me,' said Webster. Two of us crawled out and down the hill, then Whoosh

Gunner Milligan (22) after only 5 days in action

Kerboooommm. Christ, we were caught in the open! 'Our father who art in heaven . . .' I started. A German smoke bomb dropped fifty yards to our left, it was a repeat performance of yesterday. The Stukas tumbled out of the sky. 'We're in the bombing zone,' I shouted. 'You think I don't know,' says Shapiro. One by one the Stukas peeled off. 'Are you insured Shap?'

'For everything but this,' he said.

The first stick of bombs fell along the crest of the hill, right in the middle of the London Irish again. I couldn't resist looking up and watching the slow almost lazy majesty of the Stukas as they went on their nose for the final dive. It was all over as quickly as it started. We got up and ran, to the bottom of the hill, seeking safety in a wadi. I tapped into the line in case the bombing had damaged it. It was OK. Webster appeared. 'You lousy buggers! You pissed off and left me.'

'Rubbish,' I said. 'You stayed behind and left us.' After a smoke, we limbered up and set off back. I remember we didn't talk much this time. Perhaps that built-in count down had started to tick in our heads; each shell that missed you brought the one that killed you one shell nearer.

Back at the guns, the *Monkey truck was up from Waggon Lines and me old mate Edgington and I had a get together, Alf Fildes got his guitar out. Sitting in our hut we played a little jazz, Harry minus piano improvised a double bass, making a megaphone out of some artillery board paper. There and then we cooked up a song. El Aroussa.

> El Aroussa, El Aroussa,
> We'll get thru sir,
> To El Aroussa,
> No more dryin', no more tryin'
> No more dyin' for El Aroussa.
> Up and Down Lorry Carry me thru
> In out, watch out, 88's out of the blue!
> El Aroussa, El Aroussa,
> We've got thru sir, to El Aroussa.

German soldier praying for Gunner Milligan to stop playing the trumpet at night

* Monkey. Maintenance Truck for Telephone Wires.

Crappy, isn't it? Now you know why the war took so long. Don't ask me *how* we ever learned 'Lili Marlene', but the wartime grapevine was highly efficient. Here was a song the Afrika Korps brought over, the Eighth Army picked up and now we knew it. Some lads joined in singing, the guns started up, it all sounded very very strange. We played a few more boring requests, like 'Stay in my Arms Cinderella' or 'The Greatest Mistake of my Life'. Edgington and I did our routine.

'Do you know the Greatest Mistake of my Life?'
'Yes, you are.'
'Do you know "When the Poppies Bloom Again"?'
'Yes, mid April till March . . .'
'Do you know "I'll be seeing you"?'
'Not if I see you first!'

Hitlergram No. 3961

Scene: The Eagles Nest, Bertchesgarten, the Wagner Concert Hall. Stage curtains closed. Assembled are the Western World Press. House lights down. Over the speaker a voice.

Voice: 'Hello dere Vestern Vorld Gerpressen. Now! For your delight der All Deuscherband Hots shots!'

From behind the curtains comes the sound of a quartet playing a very dodgy version of 'Tiger Rag' – the curtains part – there, revealed in white monkey jackets, black trousers are a four-piece band – Martin Bormann dressed as Tommy Dorsey walks to mike.

BORMANN: 'Vell hello zer Western Press, let me make introductions – on Piano Adolph "Jerry Roll" Eichman.'

Storms of recorded applause stolen from Benny Goodman Hall Concert.

BORMANN: 'On Drums und Vibes! "Herman Milt" Goering.'

Applause – Goering does quick drum break – throws sticks in air – misses.

BORMANN: 'Ach zer practice you vill make after school hein? Ha! Ha! Now zen, rated No. 1 cripple of zer year on G Banjo und ace crooner – Slim Goebbels!'

Goebbels does hot break on banjo.

BORMANN: 'A slick trick, hein? Cool it daddy! Now! on Cornet, lead and scat vocals – zer leader of zer Reich, Adolph "Bix" Hitler!' Storm of recorded

zeigheils. The quarter launch into 'Is you is or is you ain't my baby'.

HITLER: (singing) '"Is you iss, or is you vas mein baby".'

GOERING: 'Ya!'

HITLER: 'Is you is or not mein baby now! Hein?'

GOERING: 'Crazy Daddy! Vant a smoke?'

The vocal concluded, rallentando.
Storms of recorded applause.

BORMANN: 'Cool it Herren volks!'

Martin Bormann signals, a thousand Doberman Pincer dogs surround the Reporters.

BORMANN: 'Now kids, any questions.'

The Times correspondent stands.

TIMES: 'Good evening – this new venture by the leaders of the Third Reich – what do you hope to achieve?'

GOEBBELS: 'I vill answer zis! Ya – it is new scene man – Gone ist zer goose-step – all zat crap is out, out, out man, old Ger-hat, in comes zer new Swingen Turd Reich – Unter der Linden Plattz Von-step.'

HITLER: Yea Goebbels baby!

GOEBBELS: 'Right on Daddy. Zis is zer *new* Hitler! a smile, a song, a Stalingrad!'

TIMES: 'Mr Goebbels, what started this new sound?'

HITLER: 'Me!! Ve heard zat eine Englisher Battery by zer name of "D" has got zer "Schwing Band", and zey play in zer front line. Shit men! Zey can't get away vis

zat! Zer Hitler Hot Shots vill give zer lie! OK Boys
1-2-3-4.'

Hitler launches into a growl cornet solo, 'It must be
Jelly cause Jam don't shake like that.' Flash-bulbs
explode — Martin Bormann takes the mike.

BORMANN: 'Well you folks in zer U.S.A., zis is a broad-
cast from Germany zer home of good Jazz, you have
been listening to "Bix" Hitler and his three Reich Hot
Shots, zo, Gute nacht, and remember! — (shouts) Ve
vill destroy you!'

The Mediums in front of our guns now opened up, we were all firing at an alarming rate. There was a strange tension in the air. Our O.P. had spotted concentrations of vehicle borne Infantry and Mark III German tanks moving left behind the cover of Grandstand Hill.

In burst Dawson. 'Come on,' he said. 'There's fucking Germans on the other side of this hill and nothing in between them and us! I want you, you, you, you and you,' his finger stabbed in the directions of the victims. 'Small Arms, outside now,' and he was gone. Led by Major Chater Jack, the party climbed Grandstand Hill. We at the G.P. got straffed by a lone ME 109. 'The bastard,' I said. 'Get his number, we'll report him for wilful damage.'

'Geordie' Liddel replied on the Bren gun, but was miles out.

'You're a good shit-house orderly but a lousy shot,' we shouted. How Liddel complained about our references to his humble job. 'It may be shit to you, but to me it's bread and butter,' he said. As darkness fell, the O.P. reported a German patrol had 'winkled out' a Gunner O.P. to their right. Chater 'advised' our O.P. to withdraw half a mile and go back at first light. A listening post-cum-O.P. was placed forward of our guns. We had a report that 'Tiger' tanks were in our area, they weighed 90 tons. How in Christ could we stop them! 'Simple,' I said. I held up my hand. 'Tiger Tanks – Stop.'

The BBC news that night '. . . German forces are concentrating along the line of the Medjez-el-Bab down the Medjerda Valley and towards Bou Arada . . . .'

About ten that night Jordy Dawson and Co. returned, red-eyed with whisky (where *did* he get the stuff?). 'Milligan,' he woozed, 'you can have the day off tomorrow.'

'Oh lovely, I'll drive down to Herne Bay.'

There was talk of an early stand too, so I got my head down. 0300 hours, we were awakened. 'Stand to.' I stood to.

The sound of small arms echoed around the hills. The sky was lit up by repeated flares. Towards dawn it all went quiet. The first skinny wog cockerels were crowing across the land. Lucky sods, they'd had a night's sleep. I was too tired for breakfast so went back to bed. I didn't awaken till 11 o'clock.

Gunner Milligan defending Tunis from a hole in the ground – note plenty of space in case of swollen ankles

I was desperate for a bath. The river Siliana was about a thousand yards to the rear of our position, so I took soap, towel, Tommy gun and went. It was a slow flowing river, about sixty feet across, the water was clean. I walked along the bank until I came to an access spot. I stripped, and dived in. The water was just the right side of cold to make it refreshing. Standing waist deep in the water, alone, I felt like some bird freed from a cage. I swam across then back again. 'FREE! FREE! FREE!' I shouted. I finally got out, and dressed. As I climbed up the bank, a herd of goats came over the top and swarmed each side, and smothered me in dust. I walked back very slowly, smoking, and thinking that this was all bloody mad.

'What's going on,' I asked Birch who was oiling his rifle.

'Everything,' he said, without looking up. 'Where you been?'

'I had a bath in the river.'

'What river?'

'It's about a quarter of a mile that way, you can't miss it, you keep going and when you get wet, that's it.'

I was off duty and therefore not eligible to be killed. That afternoon, with the battle all around, some silly sod says 'Test your wireless sets.'

Syd Price and I set our trucks twenty yards apart.

Syd: Hello are you hearing me? Over.

Me: Yes, hearing you strength ten – but I can hear you without the set on. This is all bloody silly. Over.

Him: Have you got any pipe tobacco left? Over.

Me: . . . .

Him: Hello Spike, can you hear me? Over.

Me: Hello Sid, what is it?

Him: Listen, Milligan you can bloody hear me, I'm coming over.

Before he arrived I managed to stuff all my tobacco into the pipe and smoke a good three pounds before he arrived to find me unconscious over my set, dying of nicotine poisoning. Now I'm not mean, but Price had a pipe, the bowl of which he hid in during air raids. A Syd Price tobacco refill meant three cargo ships.

By eight o'clock I was very sleepy so I turned in.

1400 hours and the bloody stand to! Getting up at this hour must be something like the dead rising on Judgement Day. We were told a German patrol was behind us.

I got in my hole in the ground and cringed. To camouflage

myself I stuffed the branch of a tree in the front of my web belt. On the Grandstand Hill side, there were flares and small arms firing. Lt Goldsmith ushered from his hut. He saw the bush in the hole.

'Who is that,' he asked.

'Gunner Milligan sir.'

He walked back into his hut, a pause, the door opened, a torch shone on me, the door closed followed by hysterical laughter. Not satisfied with humiliating me, they send Gunner Woods out with a kettle, who starts to pour water into the trench.

'Mr Goldsmith says it's time you were watered.'

'Bugger off,' I said, beating him with the tree.

Tomorrow night if there was a German attack I would point out the officers' quarters *personally*!

0600: Breakfast over, Shapiro, Webster and I set off.

'I feel safer out here than at the guns,' said Webster.

Suddenly, three ME 109s roared at nought feet over O.P. Hill, we all panicked, ran in circles, crashed into each other. It was pointless to lie down. As they roared over, I came to attention and gave the Nazi salute. It saved our lives I tell you! The planes raced at speed towards El Aroussa, Ack Ack shells tracing their route. We heard their cannons firing. A mighty explosion. It was an ammo dump, smoke curled up blue-black into the sky. Now! this day, I was carrying with me my gold-plated Besson trumpet to 'fulfil a certain promise . . .'

'What certain promise?' asks Shapiro.

'I promised the Hire Purchase agent I would play this trumpet where the fighting and the repayments were thickest.' Ack Ack again – sod! They were coming back! I unslung my Tommy gun, and let fly my first rounds in anger. What a great feeling. Planes gone, excitement over, we went on checking the line till we arrived at Dead Cow Farm.* I buzzed the O.P.

Me: Everything all right sir?

Lt Goldsmith: Everything *alright*? There's a bloody war on!

Me: Yes sir – what I meant was, is everything in the war alright.

Lt Goldsmith: Yes. It's working splendidly. Any tea down there, Milligan.

Me: I can't tell you sir, careless talk costs lives.

We despatched Jock with the bottle of tea and watched as he wormed his way over the crest, backside sticking up all the way. 'If there's a sniper watching, he should be able to provide Webster with a second arsehole,' said Hart. Wheeeee Crashhhh. Wheeeee Booooom Crash . . . 88's! They were bursting just behind the crest of the O.P., it was odds on they'd spotted Webster's clumsy efforts. Wheeeeebooommmmmmm Wheeeeeeboooooomm. What was I waiting for. I unsheathed my trumpet and laying sideways I played 'Mother Macree' as a further batch of shells came over. But then, the shelling started to creep down the hill towards us,

* A farm christened by me after a dead cow lying at the front door.

and Milligan stopped playing didn't he? And Milligan packed up his trumpet and ran like bloody hell towards the wadi.

'Come back here you windy bugger,' shouted Sherwood.

'Windy buggers don't come back,' I shouted.

I returned later. Jock Webster came back on his belly.

'I didna like thart,' he said, 'I might ha got killed goin' up there.'

'That was the idea,' I said. The phone buzzed. I listened in.

O.P.: Action Left, Target! Tanks!
G.P.: Action Left, Target! Tanks!

I had never seen the real thing, so I scrambled up to the O.P. trench. Without binoculars the tanks on the plain looked like toys moving at snail's pace. Our shells were landing short, the tanks were at extreme range, and moving across our line of fire. After about twenty rounds the tanks had made cover behind a hillock to our left and the fire ceased. With that I crawled back to the Carrier, 'What happened?' asked Sherwood. 'Tanks,' I said. The effect was electric. 'Tanks?' he said sitting bolt upright. 'How many?'

'Millions,' I said. 'In fact, Tanks a Million.'

High above us a squadron of Bostons and Maurauders were heading towards Tunis, then turned right towards the Eighth Army front. Flak burst around them as they disappeared in the blue distance. While we had been frolicking at the O.P., the gun position had been having fun. Here it is recounted by Gunner Harry Edgington:

'Major Chater Jack, M.C., D.S.O., had told Sgt Dawson, "I want to test the alertness of the gun positions to possible Infantry attack which might occur during the next twenty-four hours. Get some of your off-duty signallers to put on gas capes, go out in front of the guns, then infiltrate forward through the scrub to the left of the gun positions, so me (Edgington) and six of us all put capes on and sauntered off rifles and all. We did what we were told, suddenly we appear through the bushes with our rifles at the high port. Cor blimey, when the gun crew saw us, they all rushed for their small arms dived into trenches and were about to let us have it when Sergeant Griffin recognised us, "Don't fire," we hollered, just in time to stop a massacre. He then let us have the length of his tongue.* "You silly sods! You nearly got yourselves bloody killed! are you all bloody darft!" "Yes sarge" had been the meek reply. Turns out no one had warned the gun position Sergeants of the "Stunt." But another gun position had seen another group of mysterious "enemy" among which was Bdr Jones and they got fired on didn't they? and Bdr Jones gets wounded? Christ you couldn't see their arses for dust. Anyhow it all simmered down and Chater Jack knew that the gun positions were on their toes.'

Now the *good* news! Everybody was on *all night* stand to.

---

* 6¾ inches.

Hitlergram №. 3086142

With our Führer behind the Enemy Lines

GNR HITLER: Ach! I hate zese stand-toos! I shouldn't be doing zat, I should zer Sergeant be in zer kip!

GNR WHITE: Arsoles!

HITLER: You say arsoles to *me*? In Germany I am Leader of zer Turd Reich! You are lucky I only ask you for ein Fag!

GNR WHITE: I thought you didn't smoke?

HITLER: Zat is silly bugger Goebbels propaganda — he says you must never be seen wiz zer fag on! I smoke zeben-und fünfzig fags a day! I have to hide in zer cupboard, in zer Karzi, it is not easy. I am human like anybody else, I may burn ein Jew or two, but nobody's perfect I tell you.

GNR WHITE: What about sex?

HITLER: I make mit zer shag ten times a day.

GNR WHITE: Poor Eva Braun.

HITLER: Oh, not her, I screw her in zer night, she is der greatest, we screw in zer shape of a swastika! Zen ven she plays die Valkyrie on zer Beckstein I make vid zer Back Scuttle. Zen we are dansing de Tangogerstein with ze Berlin Novelty Trio.

GNR WHITE: You look shagged out — if you're goin' ter win this war you better get some sleep.

HITLER: Ha! you little Kakhi foolen! How can I loose? Look at zese good conduct passes — 1st prize Five

String Banjo at Gratz country fair! Three times Last
Tango Champion in Paris – admit defeat Tommy!

We were told the situation was 'Grave.' What does that mean?

'How do you feel Milligan?'

'Grave sir, very grave.'

Small arms firing all around us, the night passed very slowly. I was glad to see the first light in the sky. Here my Diary takes up the story:

Feb. 26th

The storm broke at about 9.30 a.m. Our troops pushed off O.P. Hill, Lt Goldsmith and O.P. Party came back. Sergeant Dawson set up an O.P. directly on the hillock in front of our guns. Position now called 'serious', 'How do you feel now Milligan?' 'Serious sir, very serious.' Sporadic fighting all around in isolated groups. Infantry manoeuvering for position.

Major Chater Jack was anxiously awaiting orders from Div. H.Q. to move. By three in the afternoon it hadn't come, so Chater Jack took the initiative and gave the order, 'Move and Quick.' I packed everything in two minutes, piled it on Sherwood's Carrier which was moving out with Lt Goldsmith aboard.

'What's happening sir?'

'We're moving Milligan.'

'Somewhere cheaper?'

'No, quieter . . . If you see a milkman tell him no milk tomorrow.'

We were the first vehicle out. Here is another excerpt from Edgington's letter with his version of that occasion:

'Monkey-Two was bumping out of a wadi and gathering speed as I came at it, with Bill Trew, Pedlar Palmer and Jack White reaching anxiously out over the half-up tail-board, (all the equipment had just been slung in) and I finished my run with the most blood-curdling hurdle-jump to clear the tail-board sufficiently for Bill, Pedlar and Jack to grab enough of me to hold on to, and nearly tearing me cobblers off.'

I watched as the Battery pulled out. We were retracing

tracks we had originally taken from the El Aroussa road, when we reached it, Bdr Sherwood, swerving, braked his left track and turned on to the tree-lined road leading towards Bou Arada. A company of infantry were digging in along the railway bank. They were second-line defence, this was the direction Jerry wanted to come. The guns were now well across the field but, as they turned onto the road, 88 mm shells started to burst among the convoy. It was deadly accurate and miraculously they didn't hit men or charges, I watched fascinated as scarlet and purple flashes exploded under the lumbering lorries and guns.

It was a lovely warm clear day – pity someone was spoiling it. Up the line comes Sgt Dawson on his motorbike.

'I was in the middle of that bloody lot,' he said.

'It suited you,' I said.

'Anyone hurt,' said Goldsmith.

'No sir,' said Dawson.

'Well anyone annoyed then?'

The shelling stopped, we had gone half a mile when Sherwood turned right off the road, into a copse of Acacia trees, the first thing I saw was a grave, a crude cross on top, a helmet with jagged shrapnel holes. A 15 cwt truck is leaving the site, the driver stops. 'You're not staying here are you? We bin shelled out, Jerry's got this place zeroed so he can drop 'em in yer mess tins.'

'Oh good, I'll get mine ready,' I said.

The guns hove to, gunners grinning, giving thumbs up signs, behind comes Major Chater Jack, unruffled, smiling, and returning the stopper on his whisky flask. 'I'm sorry we had to move gentlemen.'

While all this had been happening, at Waggon Lines a critical situation had arisen. 'I say Soldier what's that arising, over there?'

'That sir is a Critical Situation.'

Orders for them to move had arrived at the same time Jerry tanks infiltrated from 'Tally Ho' corner; to give the vehicles a chance to get away, Captain Rand, BSM McArthur and Bdr Donaldson went north to a crest to hold off a tank attack, with pick handles, lucky for them, as the

Panzers came into view, Churchill tanks of the Derbyshire Yeomanry came through the waggon lines at speed, counter attacked, knocking out 7 Mark IIIs.

My Diary: Feb 26

'Waggon lines evacuated south of El Aroussa.' Telephone contact with Waggon Lines was down, so I was sent to open up wireless contact. I threw my gear into Doug Kidgell's lorry (who was up with the rations).

Driver Kidgell, sans tin helmet, showing utter contempt for the Germans whilst 15 miles from the front

'Mind if I drive Doug?' Of course he didn't, I took the wheel, put my foot down.

'What's the bleedin' 'hurry?' says Kidgell hanging on grimly.

'I want to live,' I said raising one eyebrow like John Barrymore and crossing my eyes. 'I'm young! Lovely! I want to feel the wind of this giant continent blowing through my hair,' I laughed 'Happy darling?' I said as Kidgell shot two feet up, hitting his nut on the roof.

'Slow down! Fer Christ sake!!!'

'*He's* not in the back is he?'

'Milligan, stop! Or the child will be born premature.'

'If you saw Jerry's artillery back there, you'd realise I'm not doing this for fun!'

'I didn't say it was fun,' he raged.

We hit a large pothole, Kidgell goes up, while he's up we hit another pothole, so while he's on his way down the seat is on its way up to meet him, this time he does a semi-somersault, I have to brake suddenly and there on the floor in the shape of a granny-knot is Kidgell.

We raced past El Aroussa station – now we were safe from Jerry's artillery, I slowed.

'Who taught you to drive?' said Kidgell.

'Eileen Joyce.'

'She's a pianist.'

'That was the trouble.'

We arrived at Waggon Lines at five o'clock, too late to bivvy, so I kipped down in the back of Kidgell's lorry.

27th Feb.: First day at Waggon Lines.

0700. After breakfast, Bombardier/Artificer Donaldson detailed five men to accompany him to the old Waggon Lines to collect equipment left behind in yesterday's panic.

We drove in silence, except for me whistling, which I often did. It was an innocent pastime, free of malice, honest fun, it just drove people mad that's all. In the Carrier with me was Shit-house Orderly Forrest, he was illiterate, but didn't know that because he couldn't read or write. He had a girl in Bradford called Enid – and in reply to her simple letters we would reply on behalf of Forrest, 'Oh dearest Radiant light of Love, here, where I am serving my monarch and country, a great Symphony-like yearning burgeons within me whenever I think of you. Enid! The name is magic – and your face – whenever I sprinkle the quick lime over the crap, it's your dear face I see.' She never wrote again.

Whistling merrily we arrived at the deserted Waggon Lines. Laying around were the bric-à-brac of hasty evacuation. 'Throw it on the lorry then let's piss off,' said Donaldson, walking up hill. 'I'm going up on ridge to keep KV.'

'Where's the piano?' I said to Forrest.

'What piano?' said the blank face of Forrest.

'The Regimental one.'

'The Regimental piano?'

'Yes, where is it?'

'I don't know. You're not jokin' are you?'

'Joke? About the Regimental piano? You've never seen us playing without a piano!'

'No.'

'Well, until it's found there's no more dances, if the Germans have captured that piano we're finished.'

We threw the last of the salvage on the lorry. 'OK Bom,' I called up to Donaldson, 'you can come down, all the work's done.' The return drive was uneventful except the look the boys gave Forrest when he said 'I wonder what happened to the piano then.'

At Waggon Lines, I shared a tent with BSM McArthur, a regular but only five foot six and a half which made him lack authority to anybody five foot seven and a half. He had a face the shape of a pear held upside down. Smoke blue eyes, a straight fleshy nose, under this hung a brown handlebar moustache. Head on he looked like a motor-bike. He had advanced piles and slept face downwards. He greeted me with 'Good news you've been promoted to Lance Bombardier.' I wasn't expecting this, but was quick to capitalise, 'We non-commissioned officers must stick together. Wait till tomorrow, I'll put this bloody lot through their paces.' He was new to the Regiment having joined a week before sailing. Apparently he had gained the disfavour of someone, and been banished to Waggon Lines as a Khaki Limbo. That night he talked, I thought *I* was a Walter Mitty, but this man was a congenital liar. He started, 'I am born of noble birth, my forebears were Scottish Barons, I have Royal Blood, one of my forebears slept with Prince Charlie, from that a child was born, I am in direct line from that union.'

'Jolly good,' I said, I mean what else can you say to a short sallow Herbert, lying face downwards under three grotty blankets, total value three pounds ten. He didn't stop there. There were the yachts, 'I have one tied up at the Pool of London.'

'Oh yes, if I had one *I'd* tie it up,' I said.

'You see I married a millionairess,' he said lighting a dog-end.

'Why didn't she buy you out?'

'Oh no! I couldn't let the old country down.'

'Why not,' I said. 'Everyone else has.' He was still rambling on when I fell asleep.

Next day I dug a slit trench, roofed it with a small tent and installed the wireless, the Gun position was nearly fourteen miles away, 'If we move any further, we'll have to get in touch by medium.'

Through the daylight hours I would contact the G.P. every hour. We had a sudden outbreak of the squitters, and Gunner Forrest had to dig a second latrine to take the overflow. We all had it very bad, and no one dare go more than twenty seconds away from the Karzi without jeopardizing under-wear.

A three man latrine with two men in support

The M.O. gave us all some foul tasting pills that left you feeling like you'd slept with an Arab's toe in your mouth. After a few days it all cleared up, but during the attack Bombardier Marsden ran a sweepstake, BSM McArthur swept the pool with twenty-four visits in eight hours, he got two hundred francs and a sore arse.

My Diary: 28 Feb. 1943:

Torrential rain. Wireless trench flooded.

Contacted Gun Position.
Milligan: Hello! Tell Sergeant Dawson I need a relief.
Gun Position: Who do you want?
Milligan: Paulette Goddard.
Gun Position: What will be her duties?
Milligan: Me.

The rain! Not only did it come down, it went up 6 feet, and then came down a second time.

B.S.M. McArthur telling a gunner he owns all the mud in Tunisia

'It's good for the crops,' said McArthur.

'I haven't got any,' I said.

'I have. I've got a hundred acres in Somerset and three hundred in Canada.'

'It's not raining there.'

'I know' he said, pacing up and down, 'and it's very very worrying.'

March

Germans launched an offensive called 'Ocksenkopf'.* It went from 26 February to 5 March. They nearly broke through at Hunt's Gap, but an incredible resistance by 5 Hampshires and 155 Bty RA for over twelve hours (the latter were finally overwhelmed), decimated the Bosch so much – he had to stop.

March 13 1943: Early closing in Lewisham.

* 'Ox Head'. With names like that for a major offensive, they just couldn't have had a sense of humour.

U.S. BULLETIN

The scene: A highly camouflaged American Ice-cream refrigerator in the battle zone. A 'phone rings.

EISENHOWER: Who is that?

VOICE: I'm General Patton 2nd in line to John Wayne . . .

EISENHOWER: It's Ike here? We've taken a thrashing from the Germans at Kasserine.

PATTON: Germans? I'll put them on the list, but first we get rid of the Limeys!

EISENHOWER: Remember, form the Tanks into a circle – with women and kids in the middle.

12 March 1943. Q Bloke, Courtney says: 'We've got to move to a place called "Beja".' Soooo, we all start this bloody kit packing again. Finally the convoy lined up. BSM McArthur on his motorbike. 'Where's the Rolls?' I said. It was 44 miles to Beja, en route we passed a glut of POW's; without fail, we gave them Nazi salutes and morale sapping raspberries. The Germans looked baffled. Was this rabble the Army they were fighting? And what was this strange farting noise they made?

Goebbels News Flash

HITLER: Vat is dis fartung noise zer Britisher are making?

HIMMLER: Einer Raspberry-speilen.

HITLER: Raspberry-speilen? – vat is das?

HIMMLER: According to our secret agent it is einen fartung noise.

HITLER: How can einen Raspberry make zer fartung noise?

HIMMLER: It is einen mystery?

HITLER: Zat is not good enough! We must form Einer Raspberry-speil Panzer Unit. We will show zem who is *master* of zer Fartung noise.

*Gunner Milligan
showing his
unflagging belief in
his King and Country*

A mile outside Beja, on the verge of a tree lined dusty road, we parked our vehicles, draped scrim nets over them. Flanking us were fields of ripening corn that rittle-rattled in the afternoon breeze. The afternoon was good drying weather; I had to wash my denims and battle-dress trousers because they pleaded with me to. I hung them to dry, and repaired in my shirt and socks to sleep in Kidgell's lorry. I awoke to find the lorry a mile away at an Ordnance Depot about to be loaded with blankets. I was hoiked out of the back accompanied by wolf whistles from soldiers.

An RSM spotted me. 'Oi! *Yew*, 'ere, and double!' It was a rare sight, me running across a busy square. I came to an unclassic attention.

'Wot the bloody 'ell you think you're doing?'

'It was an accident sir.'

'What kind of accident?'

A sergeant at the Ordnance Depot saying "Wot the bloody 'ell you think your doing" to L/Bdr Milligan.

'Dysentery sir – I'm excused trousers during an attack.'
'If the A-rabs sees you they'll think we're all bloody queer.'
He took me to the Quarter Master's Store.
'Fix this nudist up with trousers.'
Kidgell was bent double with laughter as we drove back. 'You swine, Kidgell, I hope on your honeymoon your cobblers catch fire and roll down the bed.'

The roads were alive with reinforcements. A squadron of Churchills all spanking new were trundling towards the front – their gear stowed immaculately, Divisional signs freshly painted. Along the Beja-Oued Zaga Road we travelled, the sun was shining, the land was green, we didn't

Drawing done from back of
Truck. Camel boy near Oued Zaga March 1943   (sm)

have a care in the world, was there *really* a war on? We sang
songs, those nostalgic slushy moon-June love songs that had
fucked-up my generation. I was brought up to believe that
the answer to all problems was a red-rouged-moist-lipped
Alice Faye romance. I wasn't in a war really, I was, Robert
Taylor in 'Waterloo Bridge' – and Louise of Bexhill was
Vivien Leigh. Life was a series of weak-joked crappy dia-
logues one could hear in any Hollywood film from 1935 to
1945. If I made a wisecrack I was Lee Tracey, if I sang a
song I was Bing Crosby, if I played trumpet, Louis Armstrong – if I kissed a girl, Clarke Gable, if I was in a fight,
James Cagney – but who was I when washing out my socks?
Hollywood didn't recognise reality – the escapism was almost
evil, yet, I *was* looking for the happy ending, with Judy
Garland and Mickey Rooney marching triumphantly and
singing 'They call us Babes in Arms'. It never happened. It
never will, Hollywood sold us short. My generation have

suffered withdrawal symptoms ever since. But here we were singing gaily. It was ridiculous! A thin soldier, in outsize denim trousers held up with string singing 'You stepped out of a dream'. Doug had a new trick, on the first beat of the bar he'd hit the accelerator – and the lorry would lurch forward.

March 13th. The mail had arrived. Everyone went mad!

I had one from Mum and Dad, one from Lily, and Ohhh ArGGGGHHHHHHH! Three from Louise of Bexhill. AHGGGHHHHHHHHH. Help! I'm going blind. My father had rejoined the Army as a Captain in the RAOC. He was over fifty, but using glazier's putty, and blacking his bald head with boot polish, looked forty-nine. My brother Desmond was working as a runner-cum-slave to a press photographers in Fleet Street, and was in the middle of all

the fire raids and frequently came home smoke blackened, but whistling cheerfully. This caused mother to worry. She got Doctor O'Brien to prescribe whisky to 'relax her.' Every evening she would open the front window, sip whisky, and listen for Desmond's whistling. By the time he arrived mother was so relaxed she was stretched out in the passage.

All the mail didn't bring good news. Sgt Dale says "Ere! My missus has run off with a bleedin' Polish airman!' 'That's funny, so 'as mine. They must be short of planes.' Other letters were from Beryl Southby – a Norwood girl who had a crush on me, and one from Kay in Herstmonceaux – I must have pulled the birds in those days but I don't remember working at it, however, it got complicated, as this letter of Edgington recalls:

'Then – how about the night at the De-La-Warr Pavillion, when it took seven of us to get all your "birds" safely out of the place at the end of the evening whilst you "peeled-off" secretly with the eighth – the latest! Kay, the dazzling blonde from Herstmonceaux who had been waiting behind the dressing-room door with a pair of scissors clutched in her hands during the interval! – Did you know about that!!!??? Doug was first man into the room in the interval and walked right into her, as Alf arrived, he was needed to help Doug in the struggle to "unarm" her and as I came in, she was crying and they were trying to mollify her . . .*

You never showed up! If you were out in the auditorium you were still taking your life in your hands for they were all there – the two Bettys among them, flexing long fingernails, even Pearl the NAAFI girl was looking very unhappy, and there was one of the sergeant's wives I remember. (It's all lies folks! S.M.) Anyway, came the finish of the evening with Jimmy, Chalky and I nervously shepherding three of them up the left-hand (as you looked out from the stage) raised aisle or gallery where all the seating was: Well, we were just getting towards the far end of it and there were some three rows of triple cinema seats already pushed up tight against the wooden wall, that overlooked the dance floor. As we were coming up to these, I saw an army boot sticking out from the mass of steel legs. There must be another one somewhere I thought. Being on the inside, nearest to the chairs, I took one step rather more quickly and stopped and turned to*

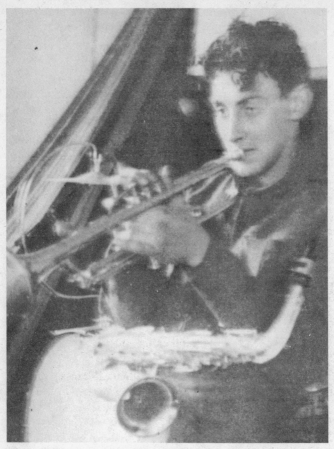

Gunner Milligan happily playing his H.P. Trumpet at De La Warr Pavilion, Bexhill, while his mates keep his birds from killing him

the girls, so as to keep their attention up at me. I risked a look down at where the head that belonged to the boot ought to be. Sure enough, there it was (at the right distance from the boot), the Milligan features all screwed up into the usual huge grinning wink. Remember? It's a pity you didn't get that one into the book, for it has, despite all *the shagging that was undoubtedly going on, a far happier and more humorous ring to it than all the other yarns about your "amours".'*

Well folks! if that's all true, I didn't know when I was well off!

Beja Waggon Lines 17 March 1943. A velvet night as against last night which was Donegal Tweed. Midnight, around me the silent, sleeping Waggon Lines, I was reading a Micky Mouse comic printed in Arabic. I shouldn't be doing this! I understood Micky Mouse, but Arabic! No, mice didn't speak Arabic. This was nonsense. I should be on the floor of the Hammersmith Palais de Danse wearing a blue chalk-stripe suit with well padded shoulders, doing the 'Suzy Q' with what's-her-name-with-the-big-boobs, who used to go out with Roy Fox's Singer, Denny Dennis, who had become the British Bing Crosby, whereas in fact, *I* was the British Bing Crosby – didn't I win the Bing Crosby contest at the Hippodrome, Lewisham, wearing a shrunken sports jacket with four and sixpenny Marks and Spencer's flannels? And again – didn't I win the EPNS solid silver Crooners Cup at the Lady Florence Institute, Deptford, singing 'East of the Sun'? and was chased frequently by the bloke who came 2nd?, anyhow, I settled down to a comparatively easy life at Beja, sitting in a hip bath and eating dates.

March 18th. We were to take returnable salvage to the RASC Depot at Souk El Khemis, Kidgell, Edgington and I, a perfect trio, all barmy, and none of us queer. On the way we stopped to exchange old battle-dresses and see through blankets with Arabs, for bunches of dates. The stickiness! By the time we got to the Depot we were stuck to each other. Kidgell had to prise his hands off the steering wheel. It was even on our boots, six feet away from the eating area!

A stark white sign with the red letters BEJA, no admission, TYPHUS.

'I wonder what Typhus is like,' said Edgington.

'Typhus is an Arab village,' I said.

'Then wot's Beja?'

'Beja is a dread disease that has struck down the people of Typhus.'

Approaching
Souk-El Khemis
drawing from Lorry

          S Millya 1943

'You notice that the Wogs don't have these diseases until
we arrive.' We drove along in silence.

   'What did one date say to another?'

   'I'm stoned.'

Souk El Khemis, was a pile of mud with windows. In the
main street we entered an Arab Café called 'Out of Bounds'.
We drank a bottle of warm Thibar white wine. Arabs in ones
and twos were seated round coffee tables. Above a three

bladed fan turned slow enough to count the blades, it was intended to disperse flies, but in fact they rode on it. We drained the bottle, and left.

Midday. Arrived at Service Corps Depot. Stopped at gates by small redcapped, two striped, military Hitler.

'Wot is yourn business?'

'I'm a Vicar's Mate but the war has spoilt it.'

'We want to play a little game do we? Gude. I like little games, now we are going to play a little game called Vicar's Mate waiting at the gate for one hour.'

'Where do they find people like him?' says Edgington.

'You take a pig's offal,' said Kidgell, 'and make it a Corporal.' Finally allowed in we drove to the salvage bay, unloaded our junk – got a receipt for it.

'Why does anybody have to sign for a load of crap like that,' says Edgington.

'Why? It puts the responsibility for all that crap onto someone else. Life is all bits of paper. You don't exist until you have a birth certificate, you are nameless unless you have a baptismal certificate, you have never been to school without a school leaving cert, you can't get insurance without a clean bill of health certificate, and, you're not legally dead without a death certificate.'

'You can't do a crap without one,' added Kidgell.

Before departing I spied a pile of American two-man puptents. I approached them respectfully, saluted, placed one under my arm and said 'This is for Wounded Knee, it's also for Wounded Teeth, Wounded Ear and Ulcerated Tongue,' one pace back, on to the lorry, and away. A brilliant tactical move, and my first blow against General Patton. The wind blew pleasantly through the lorry window. 'Did you know,' said Edgington now covered in date-sticky, 'there's a man in St John's Road, Archway who's kept a whole egg in his mouth for a year without taking it out?'

'He must be bloody mad,' I said.

'Maybe, but he's still a civilian,' he said, sliding dates down his throat. We finished the dates and felt sick.

We ourselves felt pretty free, alone, no authority, knowing

where the next meal came from, young, all that had a certain freedom too. Since then, none of us have ever felt that particular type of mental and spiritual liberty, the gall of it is, at the time we didn't know it, it appears memories always have to be forced on us. Suddenly, at an alarming speed, the skies overcast, turned black, and a thunderous torrential downpour descended. The land became a sea of reddy brown water, the force of the rain neutralized the windscreen wipers and we had to pull up.

'It will do BSM McArthur's crops in Canada good,' said Kidgell. Almost as quickly the rain stopped, the sun shone, and that peculiar musk of drying earth permeated the air, the trees were a shade greener, the air fresher. God was very good when he wanted to be. In twenty minutes the world dried out, and no trace of rain remained. 'Wot is that?' Edgington pointed to something moving along the road. We pulled up. 'There, that thing.' It was a large black scarab shaped beetle, about half the size of a matchbox. It was standing on its head and, with its hind legs, pushing a round ball the size of a small tangerine.

'That's a dung beetle.' Edgington gets out, and stands over the creature which is moving up the road.

'Why are they called Dung Beetles,' said Doug.

'Because that ball he's rolling, is dung.'

'What's he want it for?'

'He lays his eggs inside.'

'What a start in life being born up to your neck in shit.'

I picked up the beetle and placed him in a safer position where Kidgell stepped back and flattened it. We passed another batch of POWs, 'Ein Reich! Ein Führer! ein Arsole,' we shouted.

'Lucky sods,' says Kidgell, 'they're out of it.'

'Here Milligan,' says Harry with surprised recollection, 'today's St Patrick's day, any messages?'

'Yes. Fuck the English.'

That evening, I erected my new tent, and invited Edgington to share it. Suddenly the rain. 'Oh Christ,' said Harry, 'I'm on guard in five minutes,' he moaned. 'Right,' I said, 'off you go and stand in the pissing rain for your King and

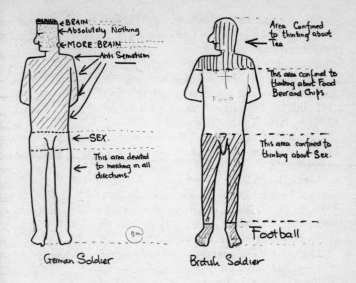

German Soldier

British Soldier

Country.' He went off groaning, and rustling in his Gas Cape. I lit the oil lamp. Now! Where were me old pornographic photographs . . . ('It's all lies officer! I bought them as art studies, I am a keen art student of twenty-one' etc.)

Pouring rain, everything was damp, cigarettes went out – matches wouldn't ignite. I was asleep when Edgington returned.

'You asleep?' he says.

'Of course I am. You don't think I always make this noise?'

'These tents were made for dwarfs.'

'I'm a dwarf, but I'm tall with it.'

'What's the bloody time?'

'The bloody time is 0200. Got a fag?'

'Yes.'

Here there was a long pause from Edgington. Mind you I took part in the pause, but it was he who started it; with great strength of character I brought the pause to an end.

'Well give us one then,' I said impatiently.

'You must make yourself clear, Milligan. If you ask me "have you *got* a fag", the answer is "yes". I *have* got a fag, but "have you got a fag for *me*," has an entirely different connotation.'

'Gis a fag or I'll break out in running sores and make 'em gallop all over you infesting your Bazolikons.'

'Is this the language of the race that gave us Joyce, Yeats, O'Casey, Old Mother Riley?'

Edge has contorted himself into the letter Z to pull his tin of cigarettes from his pocket. He hands me a curved flattened thing.

'Wot's this?'

'Players Turkish for smoking round corners.'

Edgington was going through the gyrations of getting his battle-dress off, in the confined space this meant you got his elbow in your earole every second.

'Let's face it, Edgington this is only a one man tent.'

'I *am* only one man.'

'But *I* was only one man *first*.'

'Lies, *I* am the first only one man.'

Finally we settled, doused the light, rolled left and right into our blankets. Up front the Germans had opened an attack all along the line. Here we slept to the sound of rain, it was a good arrangement.

19 March, 1943. I awoke in the wee small hours, but not for a wee, no! *something* was crawling on my chest, my first thought was it must be an eleven foot King Cobra, it was moving slowly down towards where women affect you most, if he bit me there, some twenty women in England would take the veil. I called very softly 'Harry ... Harry ... Harry ...' He moved and mumbled something like 'It's all right mother, I've known her three years.' 'Pay Parade!' I said. This got his eyes open. 'Now listen! There's something on my chest.'

'They're called blankets.'

'I'm serious, it's moving downwards, can you carefully take the blankets back and get it?' He lit the oil lamp, and very carefully peeled off the blankets, he gasped.

'Cor bloody hell!'

'Never mind that, what is it?'

'A black scorpion.'

'Rubbish, it's an eleven foot King Cobra!'

'It's a two inch scorpion. I'm going to knock it to your side.'

'What's wrong with yours.'

With a sweeping movement he whisked the scorpion off, smashed the tent pole, collapsed the tent, extinguished the light, spilled the paraffin, and set fire to the blankets. From then on the evening lost its splendour, we stood in the pouring rain amid smouldering blankets, trying to avoid the scorpion, and to retrieve our kit. The night was spent in the gay carefree interior of Kidgell's lorry.

'You clumsy bugger you wrecked our little love nest.'

'Thank you very much, next time you knock your own bloody scorpions off.'

'It was an eleven foot King Cobra!'

March 22. The morning of March the 22nd dawned. The rain had stopped. Sol ascended. We strung our damp gear

Interior of my one man tent

on a makeshift clothes line. 'Milligan! pack your kit, you're going up the line,' said BQMS Courtney.

'But me kit's soaking wet!'

'Stop the war, Mr Milligan's kit is wet.'

I massaged my steaming belongings into my kit bag, and boarded the Ration Truck with Driver Wilson. 'What's all these blood stains in the back?' I said, 'It's not the old trouble?'

'Last night, I was driving back from the Guns, I found a Don R laying by the road with his legs nearly off, a Jerry patrol had got him with a machine pistol.'

Wilson was a dour Scot, sporting pebble glasses (only the British Army would make him a driver). I think he drove in Braille. In peace time he'd been a shepherd. He rarely spoke, but sometimes in his sleep, he bleated.

'Where you taking me?'

'Munchar.'

'Munchar?'

'Munchar. It's a bombed village.'

So it was. I was to relieve L/Bdr Wenham at the Command Post. He'd come up in strange splotches and was reporting sick. Munchar was a French Colonial Farming village now deserted. The whole village lay in the shadow of Djbel Munchar, a gigantic razor-backed rock, looking like a

Djbel Munchar by Edgington

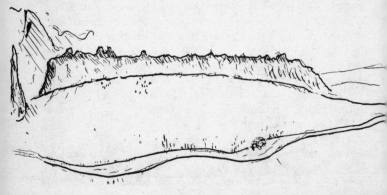

132

fossilized Dinosaur, cast by nature in grey-white granite, it reflected the colours of the day, pink at dawn, blazing white at noon, scarlet at sunset. By moonlight it looked awesome, like the hump of a colossal white killer whale, beyond it, waiting, lay the enemy. I arrived about 9.30 a.m., the truck waited to take the ailing Wenham back, he was covered in dabs of some purple medicine. 'It's lurgi' he grinned throwing his kit in the back. 'You'll like it here,' he said, 'we've done fuck all for 3 days, and it's been pissing down.'

'Now the bad news?'

'I've tested the set, the Dags are charged, the Don 5 is working, all you got to do is play with yourself and drink tea.'

The billet was a bombed farm house, minus a roof, but the first floor kept off the rain. I entered the building. Inside was a room about 20 ft x 20, to the left a burnt staircase. Lying on the floor were two of the flowers of English manhood, Gunner Arthur Tume and Gunner Payne.

'Hello Spike,' says Tume, 'I'm just reading the Daily Mirror.'

'You always were a daredevil.'

'You'll be glad to know that they've evacuated all our lads safely from Dunkirk.'

'Thank God, one of them owes me money.'

I dumped my kit in the corner. 'Who's on duty,' I said. 'I am,' said Payne, 'I've got my tin hat on.' He was cleaning his nails with a small hammer. 'As you're both lying down I think I can break the news, I am now Lance Bombardier Milligan.' Tume lowered his newspaper, 'Oh Christ no.' The 'phone buzzed, 'Hello,' said Payne, '19 Battery-all-action-packed Command Post. What? Yes, he's arrived, and he says he's a Lance Bombardier.' There was a howl of laughter from the other end and Payne hung up.

The overcast sky was clearing and the sun shone. I reported to Lt Budden, who had one of the 'rooms.'

'Ah Gunner Milligan.'

'It's Bombardier Milligan now sir.'

'Bombardier?' He turned and looked out the window. 'Oh dear' he said. 'I'll put you in the picture. We're in support of the O.P.,' he laid out a map, and indicated the spot, 'Lt

Goldsmith and Bombardier Deans are up there, where the tea stain is, they're pissed out of their minds. *We* are the carrying party for food, ammo, mail, fresh batteries, line testing and relief.'

'Do we have to take the dog for a walk as well?'

The floor was the bed, and while I was down there I did a rough pencil drawing that survived, though it's so faint I've had to ink it over.

I spent the morning exploring the house, burnt stairs (still strong enough to support one), to the First Floor, pitiful traces of happier days, a lady's slipper, a burnt doll, some women's magazines, a prayer book in French, and of all things, still hanging on the wall, a picture of M. Renaud. But lo! and

Drawing – Inside Billet – Munchar

behold in the room at the back was a piano, still playable but the floor adjacent had given way, so, I made no effort to play my attractive version of Chopsticks, which is not better than any other version, except I do it blindfolded standing on one leg with my trousers down. Oh I know it would mean nothing at a Chopin recital, but it had been well received in the NAAFI Canteen on Christmas Eve 1942, and who's to say, during those long nights at the Carthusian Monastery in the Valedemosa, Chopin didn't drop his trousers to compose the E Minor Nocturne? It was common knowledge that when he played in the relative minor of C, his legs over-heated, at one time George Sands' hands were a mass of burns.

One afternoon the line-laying truck (M2) halted by the door, and a long thing called Harry Edgington drew nigh, giving our special 'choked scream'. I greeted him in my draws cellular. (I was counting my legs to see how near to Chopin I could get.) 'And why,' he said, wriggling his fingers in the air, 'are you in a state of dishabille?'

'I'm practising to be Chopin's legs.'

'Good, I'm training to be George Sands' teeth.'

I told him about the piano, gleefully he ascended the blackened stairs as I dressed, I heard Edgington plunge into the keyboard, Big Fat Romantic chords G aug 9th + 11th + 13th – then, the music stopped, and started but now, very sad, I climbed the stairs and found him with the burnt doll propped on the music stand.

'Blimey, this *is* sad,' he said taking the burnt doll in his hands. 'It says the whole war. Ahh!' he said, 'you've brought your trumpet, great, what is it? Honey Suckle?' I nodded. As I drew near the piano it became apparent, the sagging would not take our combined weight. So! There was the strange scene of Edgington and piano in the far corner and me in the doorway blowing a trumpet. We played a few of our favourite tunes. 'What's new', 'Have you met Miss Jones?' A loud beeping from M2 Truck signalled the call for Edgington's return. 'Come on Paderewski!' came the irreverent voice of 'Pedlar' Palmer. 'Hitler wants you to tune his piano!'

Hitlergram No. 3369

The Scene: Midnight at Berchesgarten. In bed are A. Hitler, Eva Braun and her mother. The light goes on.

HITLER: Vy is zat man saying mine name?

EVA: Your fame is spreading darlink, zat man was in Africa!

HITLER: Tell zat old boiler your mudder dat!

HITLER'S MOTHER-IN-LAW: I heard you, you schwine! Zo zey know your name in Aftica, Russia, England, but you still have not given it to mein dear little Eva. (bursts into tears.)

HITLER: Stop zat crying, or I promote you to Father-in-Law.

Monkey 2 truck bumped and bounced away. Harry in the back, hat on sideways, posed eyes crossed, shouting –

'I *am* Napoleon, I tell you I *AM*.'

'You know Milligan,' said Lt Budden, 'One of these days someone's going to believe him.'

'I believe him sir.'

From the back room came the most terrifying tearing of wood, falling of masonry and the most God-awful crash, followed by swearing and twanging. The piano had fallen thru' the floor into the Batman's room, *just* missing Gunner Pill who was polishing his boots when the instrument arrived at his side.

We rushed in to see him covered in dust, a gaping hole in the ceiling – the ruins of a French Colonial Piano on the floor.

'Cor, bloody hell,' said the astonished Pill.

'You never told me you were musical,' I said. Under the circumstances his reply was remarkably controlled, 'Just missed my fuckin' 'ead!'

It's not often we had been detailed to : –

'Clean up that mess of French Colonial Piano.'

The area abounded with hot springs. To utilise this resource we dug a huge hole, dropped a canvas gun sheet in and diverted the waters thereto. One day, I observed a Gunner bathing in it when it rained, at which he rushed from the water to take shelter. Early one sunny morning, some fifty yards from the billet, skulking in the long grass was a canine-like creature, 'Are there any wolves in Tunisia sir' I asked Budden.

'There are *no* wolves in Tunisia Milligan' said Lt Budden looking at me very strangely. Through binoculars I saw it was a dog, a cross between an Alsatian and a Something Hairy. He was very thin, but then by God so was I. Every night I put some bully beef on a plate and left it out for him, and every night he would eat it, save for the nights I went out and ate it myself, I got hungry too. After a few days the dog had enough confidence to let us all touch him. He was nervous about coming into the house so I knocked up a kennel for him. I made it so nice, Gunner Tume asked if he could sleep in it and the dog sleep in his room. We named him Havelock Ellis, don't ask me why.

Lt Budden enters from his room, his face almost obscured with shaving soap.

'Is today the 26th or 27th,' he said.

'It's the 25th sir, you are at this moment shaving, your name is Lt Cecil Budden and – I know there are no wolves in Tunisia.' He peered at me. He had cut himself in several places, 'Am I bleeding,' he said, 'Yes sir,' I said 'you are bleeding awful.' He walked vaguely round the room pouring blood and humming a Bach air, then exited. Between snatches of Bach he was speaking to Havelock, 'There, did darling like that biscuit?' This was followed by growling, 'Milligan, this dog is still half wild.'

'Well only stroke the other half' I said, 'In any case your Bach is worse than his bite.'

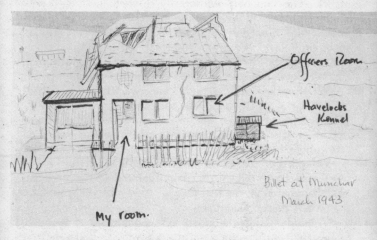

Officers Room

Havelocks Kennel

Billet at Munchar March 1943

My room.

29 March. Night. Loaded with supplies, I drove the Bren Carrier in torrential rain towards our O.P. on Frenchman's Hill. Next to me, a sodden cigarette in his mouth sat Lt Budden. 'I'm not looking forward to relieving Tony' he said. I did not like driving at night because I suffered with night blindness. I kept walking into things, falling down holes and treading on sleeping comrades. I had trodden on Gunner Maunders so many times he asked me, should he change his name to Axminster, but, this night I didn't tread on Gunner Maunders, no, I just drove straight into a Minefield. 'Don't worry' I said 'It's one of ours.'

'For God's sake Milligan' said Budden 'You've only just been promoted.'

'I'm sorry sir, a wolf ran across the road.'

Using the massed cigarette lighters of the occupants, I backed out of the danger.

'I see where I went wrong . . . I should have stayed a civilian.' With every one praying for Divine guidance we arrived at the foot of Frenchmans Hill. 'If this is his foot, he must be a big feller, ha ha ha ha ha ha,' I said. We loaded ourselves with rations and batteries and set off along a goat track. The rain had temporarily stopped, inviting Verey lights into the sky. We were all soaked to the skin and bloody miserable. 'Someone up there doesn't like us very much,' said Ernie Hart. 'Someone down here doesn't like him very much,' I said, 'I think it's on the cards that God is a German.'

'Who ever he is, he's got a weak bladder.'

We stumbled and fell, sometimes we fell and stumbled which is exactly the same only the other way around (Eh?) We reached a swollen stream and crossed it on a narrow plank of wood, with Hart halfway across the plank started to wobble, but by using his superb balancing skill, he fell in.

We toiled up the final slopes and eventually arrived at the O.P. trench covered with a tent and camouflaged with brush. We hammered on the tent pole.

'Who's there?' said a voice.

'A band of Highly Trained Nymphomaniacs.'

The tent flap flew open and an unshaven face that appeared to belong to Bombardier Deans appeared. 'Ah. You must be the one that goes round frightening little children,' I said.

We all squeezed into the tiny dugout. Hart, saturated, sat quietly steaming.

'I see you brought your own water with you,' said Lt Goldsmith. He opened his new bottle of whisky, took a swig, passed the bottle saying 'Anyone for gingivitis?' We sat cramped, passing the bottle to and fro, I was on the fro side and didn't see much of it. We passed what little news we had, smoked our cigarettes, waited for the rain to stop but no, out into it we slithered, retracing our steps to the Bren, by midnight we were back at the G.P. billet with a very weary Lt Goldsmith and a pissed Bdr Deans who were welcomed back by a snarling 'Havelock Ellis.' 'Who does he belong to,' said Deans, 'Himmler?'

April

Mussolini-Gram

April 1st
Kitchen the Fascist H.Q. Via Veneto. Count Ciano, Claretta Petacci, they are eating Spaghetti. Mussolini has just been told of the Italian surrender.

MUSSOLINI: Mamma mia! Dat-a Montgomery, he knocka-da shit outta my lov-ar-lee Ara-mee!

CLARETTA PETACCI: Neveva-minda, coma to bed, Jig-a-Jig.

MUSSOLINI: It's dat-a-swine, Church-a-hill, it is alla his-a faulta! Wata-can I-a-do!

PETACCI: Come-a-to-bed. Jig-a-Jig.

COUNT CIANO: Hava some more-a Spaghetti!

MUSSOLINI: Calla-da-Pope — musta pray for-a-my Army to knocka da shit outa da British.

PETACCI: Coma-to-bed Jig-a-Jig.

Air Raid Sirens

MUSSOLINI: Quick — under da table.

PETACCI: Itsa-aeasier-in-a-da-bed.
A bomb explodes 12 miles away.

MUSSOLINI: Quick — give-a-me another Medal.

COUNT CIANO: (crying) I want my Mamma.

MUSSOLINI: Oh-shita!

PETACCI: Jig-a-Jig!

The war was now an accepted daily routine, we had 'periods of utter boredom then bursts of sudden excitement,' as Colonel Grant had told us, from then on we went about saying 'Hello Dick, are you in an "utter boredom period"?'

'Oh no. I'm right in the middle of "Sudden burst of excitement."'

My own deranged friend Edgington wakes me up at dawn, saying 'I've just come off guard and I'm having a sudden burst of excitement.' Of course, when it came to those sudden bursts Colonel Grant got his share. On April first he was bitten by an Arab Dog, and rushed back to England barking and foaming at the mouth, some say he's still in Battersea Dogs Home.

Colonel Grant: Let me out of this pen! I tell you I'm a
    Colonel in the Royal Artillery!
Attendant: Sorry sir, according to our records you are a stray
    Arab dog, some seventy years old.

The night of April 4th the rain was thundering down, we heard Havelock suddenly barking and snarling, there was a pistol shot. I doused the light, grabbed Tommy Gun, got out the back door, Jerry patrols were famous for throwing grenades into rooms. A long figure at the front door was saying 'Pleese open ze door.' Someone said 'It's Charles Boyer!' It was the French farmer who owned the house, he had come back to ask us if we'd seen his dog, which was in fact Havelock Ellis who, in the dark had attacked him, and the Frenchman had shot him.

We found Havelock in his kennel, a bullet in the head. God knows how he managed to get back, it's the homing instinct, even if it's only made from charge cases. We were all broken up about it. The Frenchman had brought us a bottle of wine. We drank it and cheered up a bit. Lt Goldsmith invited us all into his room, where he opened up his whisky. Alf Fildes got his guitar out, and I played 'Parlez-moi d'amour' on my trumpet. A strange evening, but then, weren't they all? Next day we buried Havelock. I washed the blood off his face. We lined a large charge case with an old blanket, dug a respectably deep grave. Over it we mounted a board, and I wrote,

Here lies the body
of Havelock the Dog
Shot in the head
And dropped like a log.

He was a very Good dog.

April 1943

I suppose he's still there.

April 6th 1943. Battery Diary:

Battery Commander to Sidi Mahmond O.P. as C.R.A. Dep for 71 Field Arty: Group.

Munchar C.P. 08.00 hours. Pouring rain, and other things. Sgt 'Georgie' Dawson's motorbike arrives which he drives straight into the room. 'There's going to be a big party tonight,' he grinned.

'A party?' I said, 'I can't go, I haven't a thing to wear!'

'Good, it's for nudists.' He proceeded to give details;

Major Chater Jack, Gunner Woods, Gunner Tume, L/Bdr Milligan (oh shit), Bombardier Edwards, OPAck* and Bombardier Andrews from the recently arrived 54 Heavy Regiment. 'He's coming along for the experience,' said Dawson. He grinned evilly. It was deluging. The rain dripped in from every crack and seeped over the door sill.

'The wireless truck will collect you at 19.00 hours.'

'19.00?' I said. 'That's a pity, my watch only goes up to 12.' He passed a damp cigarette. 'Ta,' I said. 'I'll have it valued later.' I donned my Gas Cape and with Dawson, prepared to dash from the cookhouse. 'Right *now*!' yelled Dawson. Giving Red Indian War whoops we splashed across.

Fuck! Fuck! Fuck! I'd left my bloody mess tins behind. 'Borrow mine,' says 'Smudger' Smith licking his tins clean.

---

* Observation Post Assistant.

The room was a dark, damp, mess of muddy gunners, all chomping away at breakfast; all very gloomy.

'Hands up those who haven't been killed yet,' I said cheerily. The replies were 'Get stuffed, Bollocks, and Up Yours,' a grand bunch of lads. 'Good news men,' said a mud soaked creature, 'Look,' he held open a Radio Times and pointed to this.

DANCING CLUB

Victor Silvester, well-known band-leader and dance expert, writes of his new series, 'BBC Dancing Club'. It starts in the Forces programme on Wednesday.

'Oh hooray,' I said, and grabbing Gunner Tume, I swept him into an ankle deep mud-waltz. 'God you look lovely Gunner Tume!' I said. 'Get stuffed' he said breaking free.

Hitlergram No. 361

The scene: The Eagles Eyrie, in the bath are Hitler, Admiral Doenitz and Goebbels. Doenitz is playing with the German Navy.

HITLER: Vat do zey mean, 'Get stuffed'.

GOEBBELS: Zey are having zer breakfast, and he is vishing zem 'get stuffed' wiz zer food.

HITLER: So, we have broken an nudder of zere codes; now, what is zer 'Bollocks' and 'Up yours'?

GOEBBELS: I do not know Führer.

HITLER: (foaming at the mouth) Vhy don't you know, you little crippled creep!

He smashes the bath water with his fists and hits Doenitz below the plimsoll line.

ADMIRAL DOENITZ: Ach – mein bollocks!!

HITLER: Vonderschoen! anudder British Code has been broken! I promote you from Admiral Doenitz to Field Marshal Goering!

A knock on the door in Nazi.

HITLER: Who is zat!

VOICE: Martin Bormann, I have zer message for you.

HITLER: Slide it under the door.

Sound of Bormann grunting.

BORMANN: It won't go under.

HITLER: Vy not?

BORMANN: It's in mein head.

Hitler goes into a fury, bites his sponge to pieces, stops when he notices Goebbels doing something which will surely drive him blind.

HITLER: Stop zat! Or I'll never go to zer pictures wiz you again.

A wafer thin head covered in blood comes straining under the door.

MARTIN BORMANN: I haff done it mein Führer!

'What *can* you do?' lamented Shit-house Orderly Liddel, 'this bloody rain has flooded the Karzis, there's *Richards floating everywhere.'

* Richards = Richard the Third = Turd. Cockney rhyming slang.

Gunner Liddell inspecting the flooded latrines

We all had our troubles. Liddel was a dedicated Latrine Orderly, his twenty seaters were immaculate, the squatting pole sandpapered to a fine degree, not once was there complaints of splinters. It wasn't the subject I'd choose for breakfast but there you are.

'So, we're going to a party,' said Gnr Payne.

'Yes, it's somewhere on Sidi Mahomed.'

'That'll be easy to find in the bloody dark.'

'Don't worry. A Wog with a white stick is leading us.'

'What's for breakfast.'

'Powdered eggs.'

'Christ knows how chickens lay 'em.'

I eased into Tume's chair as he dashed off for his breakfast.

'Are you on this thing tonight?' asked Gunner Payne.

'Yes I'm going with Major Chater Jack on this thing.'

'Did he ask for you?'

'No I asked for him on this thing.'

My Diary:

6th April on this thing. Howling gale, intermittent rain. Gnr Tume, Bdr Andrews from 54 Heavy RA left at dusk. 'Chater' in high spirits (Johnnie Walker), asks me how 'Highland Laddie' goes.

Me: It goes Dum-de dum-dum-dum with intermittent rain.

Major Chater Jack: Thank you, I can manage on my own now.

We moved off at dusk into the approaching darkness, the noise of the wind making conversation difficult. I switched on the set, the red contact and the working light came alive. I donned headphones, tuned into battery network, the interference was appalling, the voice of Shapiro at the Command Post barely audible, so I went on to morse-key. The night was pitch black, the mud a foot deep with the differential constantly coming in contact with rocks. I tuned in B.B.C. News, passed spare headphones into the cab. 'Very bad reception,' shouted Chater. 'Yes sir, shall I write and complain?'

He said something, but was drowned out by the elements, 'At *once* sir!' I said smartly. Two miles on we reached Sidi

Mahmoud and started up hill. Driver Robinson puts his stamp on the evening, he lands us in a minefield. 'Sorry sir,' his squeaky voice was saying. 'I didn't know what Achtung Minen meant.'

'It means instant bloody death man!' explained Chater Jack with remarkable control. Hanging over the tailboard I directed him back on our tracks and my face was spattered with yellow mud. 'You've got mud on your face, ha ha ha ha,' said Bdr Edwards who was not noted for his wit. 'It's not mud,' I explained, 'this is what happens when the shit hits the fan.'

'How does it go again?' called Chater. I re-sang the opening bars with intermittent rain.

'Doesn't he know any other tunes,' said Edwards.

'Any *others*? Christ, he doesn't know this one, he only brings me along as an amenuensis.'

'Amenuensis?'

'It's what Eric Fenby was to Delius.'

'The dirty sod,' said Edwards who was not noted for his wit.

When we arrived at the O.P., the rain stopped but the war didn't. Chater Jack ensconced himself in a splendidly roofed O.P., on the forward slopes on Sidi Mahmoud, reached by a communication trench. There to meet him were three artillery officers from 71 Field Artillery Group, holding maps. The truck was 50 yards behind the O.P. To avoid detection, we had to run the wireless remote control to the O.P. while I stayed on the truck to relay the orders. Meanwhile Tume and Andrews dug a trench.

Midnight, the wind almost a gale. In the back of the truck we sipped tea and played twilight pontoon, me with headphones listening on the Infantry network. A silent attack was to go in and take their objectives by 04.00, we were standing by if they called for fire. At 03.50 hrs. on our right, an Artillery barrage was to support the 78 Div. attack on the Munchar-Medjez-el-Bab front. As the hour came I thought of those young men going forward into darkness towards death or mutilation. At 03.50 the sky sang with flashing lights, a thunder of iron artillery rolled through the night, my wireless came alive with urgent voices, 'Hello Baker Charlie 2, we're pinned down by mortars at Wog-Dog Farm,' every call was a life and death affair, and here I was in comparative safety.

'Hello Milligan?' it was Chater Jack. 'Yes sir – it goes Da-da-die – –'

'No, no! I want to speak to "Sunray".'*

I moved the dial towards our own net, as I did the opening bars of Bach's Toccata and Fugue filled my headphones, it was too much, I burst into tears. 'What's the matter,' said Driver Robinson.

'It's a piece of music.'

'Must be fucking 'orrible to make you cry.'

The music soared, the barrage raged on, turning the night red, green, orange, purple . . . Gunner Tume relieved me on the set. 'There's tea in the O.P.' he said.

I stumbled along the communication trench, the wind had dropped, I looked up, the sky was clearing.

* Sunray: Code name for Battery Captain.

In the dim light of the O.P. Chater Jack and three Officers were sipping tea. I saluted. To a man they ignored me. Two signallers squatting on the floor clutching telephones, writing messages and handing them to the officers who, to a man ignored them. Gunner Woods, slaving over a hot primus, filled my mug. The officers were talking, 'I don't like hybrid strains,' one was saying. 'Too much like having a queer in the

A whole band of bloody fools

garden. Ha ha ha.' 'What a crowd of bloody fools,' I thought. 'You should have come earlier,' whispered Woods, 'they were on about the price of tennis shoes.' Chater was passing his whisky flask around. Suddenly, at 04.59 the Barrage stopped. The 'phone buzzed. 'For you sir,' said a buck-toothed Signaller. 'Hello?' said Chater, 'Right.' He put the 'phone down. 'Gentlemen, the North Irish Horse are going in,' he looked at his watch. 'Dead on time,' he grinned.

'How's the attack going sir,' I ventured.

'I haven't had one yet Milligan,' he ventured. The junior officers laughed – they had to. They peered thru' the slits into the night, where a myriad permutations of muzzle-flashes told their story. Woods grinned at the sight of officers staring into the darkness with binoculars. 'They're our leaders,' he whispered, tapping his head. Dawn was emerging from our right, which was a good arrangement. Soon the battle panorama was revealed; in front, a large valley, on the far slopes, tanks of the North Irish Horse were fighting their way up Djbel Kachbia. To our left the 2nd Hamps. were attacking the slopes of Djbel Mahdi. 'We've got to get the set out of the truck,' says Tume hurriedly, 'it's got to pick up something.'

'Oh shit!'

'It could be that.'

We unloaded the set. Blast! The remote control cable wouldn't reach the slit trench. 'Oh shit II.' So we had to leave it on open ground, then, the bad news, a series of 88's burst around us, we moved at considerable speed into a trench and huddled in the bottom, I let out a yell as a piece of red hot shrapnel fell on to my hand.

'There's bloody luck!' said Tume, 'hit by the enemy and no blood.'

'My Blighty one and it didn't work,' I moaned.

Bombardier Andrews was sweating and pulling at his lower lip – I don't know why, it looked long enough.

'How long does this go on,' he said.

'Until the war is finished,' I said.

'Don't take any notice of him,' said Tume, seeing that Andrews was frightened. 'Sometimes a few minutes, sometimes an hour, it depends which *German's* on duty.' The wireless came to life, bravely Tume crawled out and put the headphones on – bravely I watched him do it. Luckily the shelling stopped. The battle was moving away. Sgt Dawson had arrived, he dismounted and let off. 'Ah, that's better,' he said. 'Only for you,' I said running clear. 'Come back you coward,' he shouted. 'It's one of ours.'

The rest of the day was a bore save for sudden rushes to hide from ME 109's and periodic visits to watch the Battle. We dined well on hot stew brought in vacuum containers. By sunset the battle had left us behind, we packed up and returned to Munchar.

A gunner piddling against the gun wheel watched by his comrades

Divertissement Sept. 1973

As I sit in a suite on the 13th Floor of the Eurobuilding in Madrid, writing this volume, I reflect on that time 30 years ago, and the emotional analysis of those khaki days, have left such a deeply etched impression, that the whole spectrum actually re-inhabits my being with such remarkable freshness that the weight of the nostalgia is almost too much to bear, feelings that I had incurred in those days, towards people, incidents, nature, which I thought of as almost trivial, were really of Titanic proportions, and ones, that I now realize were to stay fresh, and become more poignant as the years passed, and the desire to experience them all once again, be they good, bad or indifferent, became a haunting spectre that suddenly, during the course of a day, takes you unawares, a particular word, a scent, a colour, or song could trigger it off. It could be at, say, Ronnie Scott's Club with a companion. Without warning someone plays a tune, and immediately, the surroundings and the companion become total strangers, and you long for those yester-ghosts to snatch you and rush you back to that magic day it happened. I used to scoff at my father's looking forward to his annual World War I reunions, but now I know, you *have* to have them! In fact I was instrumental in getting our own D Battery reunions started, and lo and behold, the attendance increases every year.

Despite the friendships I have made since the war, it is always those early ones that have weight, understanding, confidence and mutual experience that I cling to. Though my best friend Harry Edgington has emigrated to New Zealand, we are closer than ever, I know that a particular tune will automatically make him think of the time we played it together, and the same applies to me. Our correspondence is prodigious, his letters fill 3 Boxfiles, likewise recorded tapes, in which he sends his latest compositions, asking my opinions. He sends me tapes that send me into gales of laughter and yet all these occasions are not really happy, and yet I welcome them, they give a most soul warming effect, it savours of satisfaction, and yet is emotionally inconclusive, it has become, like cocaine, addictive. Is it because with the future unknown, the present traumatic, that we find the past so secure?

April 8 1943: This way to another battle. At Sunset we drove to a rendezvous with Captain Rand, Bdr Edwards, Gunner Maunders in a Bren driven by Bdr Sherwood, it was dark when we met, 'We'll sleep here tonight,' said diminutive Captain Rand in a voice like Minnie Mouse. We slept fitfully by the roadside as trucks, tanks, etc. rumbled back and forth but inches from our heads.

April 8 1943: Djbel Mahdi. Up at first light, drove in the wake of a hurried Jerry retreat along the floor of a hot dust-choked valley, we passed still burning vehicles – some ours, some theirs. A few carbonised bodies – 'brew ups' as Tank men called it. We stopped to pin-point our position, to my left, lying face down was the body of an Italian not long dead, the blood on his neck still oozing, lovingly, I removed his

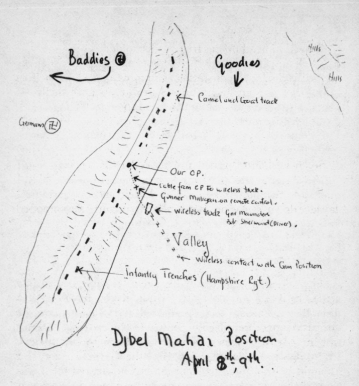

Baddies ⊕

Goodies
↓

Germans (↑↓)

← Camel and Goat track

← Our O.P.
← cable from O.P. to wireless truck.
← Gunner Mulligan on remote control.
← wireless truck Gnr Maunder
                  Bdr Sherwood (Driver).

Valley

←* Wireless contact with Gun Position

← Infantry Trenches (Hampshire Rgt.)

Djbel Mahar Position
April 8th, 9th.

watch.* The Bren stopped at the foot of Djbel Mahdi. The
2/4 Hamps were still digging in when we arrived. I followed
Capt. Rand and Bdr Edwards uphill, unreeling the remote
control from the wireless. Fuck! it didn't reach. Rand and
Edwards dropped on their bellies just below the crest. I had
to run back, fix them a telephone that reached back to the
remote control, so they shouted fire orders to me by telephone, and I passed them on by wireless. We didn't have
time to dig in, and Christ! a German 'Stonk' hit us – it was
a rain of shells. To stay where I was meant death, so I ran
to an Infantry Officers' fox-hole.

'Any room for one more?' I said.

* I gave it to my father, and it's still in my mother's possession.

158

'Sorry old boy, this is a one-man trench.'

I dived in head first as fresh shells landed.

'Well now it's a bloody two-man trench.' I tell you! They are willing to let you die rather than move over! The shelling stopped. I got out and returned to duty – more shells – I found a small depression in the lee of some rocks.

'Where are you,' shouted a voice.

'I'm in a depression,' I said.

'Aren't we all,' was the reply.

So far we hadn't passed any fire orders, it was very hot, I asked Maunders on the wireless if he had any water. Yes. I started to run down to get some. A fresh mortar barrage. I lay face down, sweating. It stopped. An infantry man stopped by me, God knows where he came from.

God: He came from the 2/4 Hampshire my son.
Me: Ta.

The soldier delighted in telling me, 'It's no good hiding there, he'll get you no matter what, if you haven't got a trench, any minute now he should start his mortars, he dropped some this morning just where you're lying.' All this got my back up (which by now was down by my ankles). 'Why don't you fuck off and join the German Army?' I thought he was going to shoot me but he cleared off. I was learning the strange quality of the human race. His kick was to find somebody who looked scared, and try and make him terrified. I suppose he liked feeling little girls' bicycle saddles as well. A Hampshire private popped his head up from a funk hole. 'If they attack, do you think we can hold 'em?' 'Yes,' I said confidently, 'there's a barrage going down at 2.'

'Oh good,' he said.

I got some water from Maunders, then dashed up to my remote control in time to pass fire orders. It was 13.59 hours. At 14.00 the barrage went over followed by the infantry attack. From the crest I watched the P.B.I. going forward, down the slopes of Djbel Mahdi, across the valley and up the slope opposite. Men fell sideways and lay still, no one stopped, they reached the German F.D.L.'s, from the distance it looked comic. Men jumping out of holes with hands up, men running behind trees, leaping out of windows; it took about an hour. By 3 o'clock we had taken the position, but Jerry counter-attacked, we shelled him, and broke up the attack. Around a hill comes a British Officer, clowning at the head of about 50 PoW's from the 1/755 Grenadier Rgt, the young officer was Goose-stepping and shouting in Cod German 'Zis is our last Territorial demand in Africa.' Be-him a stiff, bitter-faced Afrika Korp Oberlieutenant marched with all the military dignity he could muster, none of his men looked like the master-race. As they passed, our lads stood up in their fox-holes farting, and giving Nazi salutes; recalling the ritual of ancient conquerors riding on a palanquin and parading their prisoners of war behind them. Here there were shouts of 'you square-head bastards' and 'I bet we could beat you at fucking football as well.' Behind us across the valley Churchill tanks were attacking a low hill, up the valley came a squadron of FW 109's. We all let fly, we were feeling good, suddenly the leader burst into flames. Bdr Sherwood shouted 'Look Spike, look!' The plane left the formation, went on its back in a slow death agony, then raced to the hills opposite and exploded. '*Woah-ho! Mahomed' we yelled. 'That's for my brother,' said a bitter Irish voice.

We were not out of mortar range but we kept getting small

* 1st Army battle cry.

Jerry Straffing April 1943 – from ditch near Djebel Munchar

*'Stonks' of 88 mm's landing behind the crest. I suddenly heard a scream. 'I can't stand it any longer, I can't, I can't, I can't.' A young infantry lad came past, his face buried in his hands, accompanied by two old sweats. 'There, there, lad,' one was saying, as they led him away. Poor bastard, sitting in a hole in the ground, just waiting, hoping the next batch of shells won't get you. That night I slept fitfully in my shallow hole.

Trauma

I was smoking a cigarette when the mortar bomb hit me, when I regained consciousness I was lying on my side, my left shoulder and arm were lying 20 feet away, my lung was protruding from my chest, flies were swarming on it, my sight faded, even tho' I knew my eyes were open I couldn't see, talk or move. I hear the voices of stretcher bearers. Thank God, if they hurried I might have a chance. 'There's one here,' said a voice. Another voice replied, 'No, he's dead, get the wounded ones first, bring him later.'

'Spike! SPIKE!' The voice of Maunders was shouting in my headphones.

It was morning . . .

'Hello Alf. Yes?'

'Why didn't you answer?'

'I was waiting for the stretcher bearer.'

'What?'

'Nothing – what you want?'

'I've got some tea.'

'I'll be right down.'

I scrambled like a hunted beast to the bottom of the hill where all was peace. I sipped the tea luxuriously. I have never tasted the like of it before or since. The next day was reasonably quiet, but one expected 'things' to happen, I was glad when at sunset we were told to close-down O.P. as our guns were now out of range.

We packed up our gear. 'Had a nice day,' said grinning Sherwood from his 7 foot funk-hole.

* Concentrations of Artillery fire.

'Why did you stop, 3 feet more and you'd have come out on the Northern Line.'

'I think you did well today,' he said. 'I enjoyed watching you running about, you must be very fit.'

'Your turn will come Sherwood.'

'I am one of His Majesty's Military drivers and I do not partake in violence or running about like a scared rabbit, on my pay it's not worth it.'

Capt. Rand and Bombardier Edwards came down, both grinning. Strange, after sticky situations men always grinned, even burst out laughing. We climbed into the Bren. It was sunset, the land was bathed in red, the dust from our tracks looked like powdered blood, perhaps it was. Lorry loads of reinforcements passed us, some of the men were singing as they disappeared in the dusk. 'Singing songs going into battle is supposed to be old fashioned,' said Captain Rand. 'Ah,' I said, 'they don't do any fighting sir, they are especially trained singing soldiers who drive along the front line singing merry songs to keep up morale, indeed there's a great Trainee Singing Camp at Catterick, where men are selected for the vocal control under shell fire.' I went raving on, I was mad I know, under these conditions it was advisable. Darkness settled. We seemed to have been driving a long time. Rand gave a polite cough. 'Where are we Sherwood?' Sherwood gave a polite cough. 'I was just going to ask you that sir.' I gave a polite cough. 'May I be the first to congratulate you on getting lost in a world record time of 1 hour 20 minutes.'

With a failing torch, Capt. Rand perused the map. We were 7 kilometres adrift. In Stygian darkness we arrived back at Munchar. I groped my way to the Cook House. 'The Caviar's all gone,' says Cook May, 'and the Dover Sole is off.'

'It always was,' I said shovelling cold MacConockie into my face. 'I must put myself down for an MM' I added.

'Done something brave?' said May.

'Yes, I'm eating this bloody stuff.'

'Aherough!' The sound of an approaching Edgington, 'Something tells me Field Marshal Milligan is nigh,' he waffled.

'Nigh dead,' I replied.

Edgington tells me there's mail! and off-loads 3 letters and a parcel! from Mother? I'd heard of such things in Vera Lynn's songs. The parcel contained Fruit cake, a comb, holy medals, writing paper, Brylcream, 3 pairs grey socks, 3 Mars Bars, a holy picture of the Virgin Mary, 3 packets of Passing Cloud, 6 bars of soap, lovely – except when you smoked the fags they tasted of raw carbolic and you went giddy. An hour later, full of Mars Bars and wearing a necklace of holy medals and 3 pairs of grey socks, sick with soapy fags, I wearily pulled my blankets over my powerful Herculean body, and had the first good sleep I had had for 5 nights. As I lay there on that floor, Churchill was sitting in bed writing a letter to the Min. of Ag. I quote:—

I understand you have discontinued the small sugar ration which was allowed to bees . . . .

I won't go on, but supposing *I* wrote to the Min. of Ag.

Sir, I understand that you have discontinued the sugar icing that Gunner Milligan used to have on his doughnuts . . . .

At the same time the BBC were hitting the enemy pretty hard.

COMMUNITY

WHISTLING

Join in and whistle with

Ronald Gourley and the boys

this evening at 6.30

Oh how we enjoyed a good evening's whistling after being in a trench for 3 days and nights.

April 11, 1943. I awoke to a sunny morning, 9.00 a.m., a lizard was sunning himself on the window ledge. Gnr Pills did a noble thing, he brought me breakfast in bed! 'Why did you do it? You're not queer are you?' 'I don't know,' he said, 'Waitin' on orficers is a dooty, well, I was orf dooty, and I fort I'd do a good deed for the day and I seed you sleepin' and I fort, he's 'ad an 'ard time or 'eed 'ave gotten up for 'ees breakfast, so I'll get it for 'im,' then added, 'You won't tell anyone will you, or they'll all bleedin' want it.'

A bath! Ten minutes later I stood naked by the thermal spring soaping myself, singing, and waving my plonker at anyone who made rude remarks about it. 'With one as big as that you ought to be back home on Essential War Work.' It was nice to have these little unsolicited testimonials. The animal delight of sitting in a rocky pool of running warm water, under a blue sky and a brilliant sun, is one of life's bonuses.

I dried myself on what had once been a towel against what had once been a body. I was a wiry nine and a half stone. I tried to think of myself as a suntanned lean Gary Cooper but I always came out dirty white skinny Milligan. 'You look like a bag of bones held together by flesh coloured tights,' said Spiv Corvine. 'Don't go,' I said, 'stay for my description of you, you short-arsed little git!'

Letter Home:

My dear Mum, Dad, Des,

Thanks for the parcel, don't put soap in with fags. Out of action for the day, hence letter. Weather is hotting up, about 70°, it's shirt sleeves. And how silly we all look, naked except for 2 shirt sleeves! I believe they are shortly to issue Tropical Kit, or KD's (Khaki Drill) which will bring back memories of Poona. I still remember those boyhood days with remarkable clarity. I think if you enjoy a childhood, it is indelible for life. Clearest are memories of hearing the strident Bugle, and Drums of the Cheshire Regiment playing 'When we are marching to Georgia,' and the Regiment swinging by, so

My mother informing my father of the contents of my letter

impeccable, bayonets and brass buttons flashing light signals in all directions, the blinding white webbing, boots like polished basalt, trousers crackling with starch, the creases with razor edges, the marks of sweat appearing down the spines of the men, the Pariah dogs slinking from the path of the column, and, the silent resentment of watching Natives. I don't think we can retain it as part of the Empire much longer. I give it until say 1950. Can't tell you much because of Censorship; so far miraculously, no one in this Battery has been hurt by enemy action. Not much chance to play Jazz at the moment, but listen regularly to AFN Algiers. I hope my records are O.K. I put them in a box under my bed with a cardboard sheet between each record. If you move, please be very careful of them. We're billeted in a war-damaged house, it's in a bad state, and we are trying to get a reduction in our rates. I hear a distant scream saying 'Lunch will be *served in an empty cowshed,' or is it 'Cows will be served in an empty lunch shed,' so I'll be off.*

Love to you all,
your loving son,
Terry.

P.S. Send more cake, chocolate, fags, Pile ointment, but for Christ sake no more holy medals.

Last day Munchar

'Fresh flowers from the fields of Tunisia Sir.'

'Oh Milligan how nice,' beamed Lt Budden, his solemn face journeying to a smile.

'I don't like plucking flowers, but' – I recalled Lady Astor visiting Bernard Shaw, remarking it was Summer yet he had no flowers in his house. 'No mam,' he replied. 'I like flowers, I also like children, but, I do not chop their heads off and keep them in bowls around the house.' A great man. She was a twit. She filled Parliament with Bon Mots, and put progress back a hundred years.

'Put them in this,' said Lt Budden filling a broken jar with water. We placed the flowers on a rough square wooden table.

'They do brighten up the place,' said Lt Budden standing back to admire them. Christ, I thought, the English are so bloody civilized, and I made a mental note to forgive them for the dispossession of my family's farm in Ulster during The Plantation.

'I think they are Ranunculus.'

'Oh? I thought they were flowers.'

The phone rang. I beat Budden to it.

'Hello, Bdr Milligan.'

'Want any chicken shit?' said a voice.

'Who's that?' I said.

'Rhode Island Red,' a gale of laughter, then click. I suspect the joker was Bdr Sherwood, who was given to such pranks, he was one of five brothers, a first class driver, a very clean soldier, a good footballer, and a bloody awful pianist, I think it was the beer.

April 11/12. The front line is out of range. Officers are reccying new positions. The Fifth Mediums were settling into a new one on a farm when a Gun Lorry runs on a mine, it blows off the front axle, the driver jumps out to inspect damage and has his legs blown off. He bled to death before he reached hospital. Discussing it that night I said: 'It might have been a blessing in disguise that he died.'

'Oh no, no, no,' says Gunner Maunders rising from his blankets like Lazarus from the dead, but worse looking, 'people live with their legs off, there are even advantages.'

'Like what?'

'For a start he hasn't got so far to bend down.' He wasn't joking.

We rendezvoused at Map ref. 4940, a grove of ancient olive trees, and hid up all day. The terrain was rocky white outcrops, sudden valleys, chasms, tortuous for man and machine. I tuned in Allied Forces Network, round the back of the truck comes Edgington's grinning face, with a paper moustache held to his lip, otherwise he appeared to be in control.

'Arrrrg,' says he, 'this looks like the Interval for World War Two.'

'Arrg,' sez I, 'absolutely right, I'm just casting the Battle of Tunis.'

'What part do I play?'

'A crippled Grannie with identical matching plimsoles.'

He took my hand. 'You look lovely in the moonlight, Samantha,' sez he, 'What's a nice gunner like you doing in a war like this?'

'I'm the duty homosexual,' sez I. I give him a set of headphones and we listen to music until 'Tea up,' shouts a voice. Edgington leaps out the truck and nearly decapitates himself.

'Say after me,' sez I, 'I must remember to take my headphones off.'

'Nonsense!' sez he, 'it's your duty to get me a thirty-mile extension so I can wander freely with headphones on and a magnetic vanilla-flavoured truss that points due North.'

'Come in Gunner Edgington your time is up,' sez I.

The Tunisian night closed in, the sky turned pink, purple, then rapidly into a fathomless black, then, the stars, stars, stars. Dinner was nigh; we knew by the clanking mess tins of those who carried clocks in their stomachs. His name? Driver Kidgell!

'How do you time it to the second?'

'I park my lorry near the Cookhouse.'

'I suppose,' Harry said, 'after the war you'll sleep in the kitchen.'

'Kitchen?' I said, 'he'll sleep in the food. If his guts was on the outside, they'd look like worn out suit linings.'

It was sing-song night. Dvr Fildes strummed his guitar, our voices echo into the feline darkness. Lt Goldsmith joined us with two bottles of Rosé and a silly grin. 'I have

Lt Tony Goldsmith on right of picture with Derek Huason

brought along Major Chater Jack's Pink Voice Improver.'
A sort of cheer greeted this.

'I have a request,' he said.

'What is it? Shut up?'

'The Tower fer you Milligan.'

'Thank you sir, I'll move in tomorrow.'

'I have a request for you, Smudger Smith, to sing "Ole King Cole," complete with all foul and bawdy references.' Smudger stepped forward, five foot eight, chunky, blue eyes, a disarming grin (Smith! grin at those Germans and disarm them!), he was the breath of Cockney London, a Smithfield porter. He launched into song.

> 'Oh Old King Cole
> Was a merry old soul,
> A merry old soul was he
> Called for his pipe, he called for his bowl,
> And he called for his fiddlers three.'

There was a late moon, it reflected on the trunks of the olive trees standing ghost-like, their aged limbs extended like tired wooden arms. 'Did you know Harry – that ancient Greeks thought they were the tortured souls of the departed?' 'Yes, I did,' he paused. 'Ahh! it's so peaceful,' he said, puffing his cigarette. 'It makes a nice break,' I said, 'I don't like the war any more. I wish, right now, I was on the stand at St Cyprians Hall, Brockly, SE 23 and there was Jim Cherry on Alto, Billy Mercer on Tenor, and I was doing Bunny Berrigan's chorus in "Song of India", and all the little darlings are looking at me, especially Ivy Chandler, with the lovely legs. Oh roll on demob, no more bloody Woolwich Arsenal for me, it's straight to Jos Loss and asking for an audition.'

'You'd make a good chauffer.'

'Shut up! Heaven is a fourteen-piece band with me on second trumpet, and the money would be good.'

'All money *is* good,' said Edgington.

'All money is not good, take Chinese money.'

'Chinese money *is* good, *if*,' he added, 'you're Chinese.'

'It's no good being Chinese, *with* Chinese money, you can't go into Cheesmans of Lewisham, and put Chinese money down and ask for ten Woodbines or even Woodbines.'

'I was thinking of the Chinese *in* China, not bloody Cheesmans of Lewisham.'

'I say even if you're Chinese, *with* Chinese money and you go into a Chinky-poo fag shop, you still couldn't ask for 10 Woodbines.'

'Why not?'

'They don't sell Woodbines in China.'

'What proof have you got? If you say there are no Woodbines in China, you must be backed up by *facts*.'

'All right, don't shout! The baby's asleep! Now, have you ever seen a Chinaman?'

'Yes.'

'Where?'

'Limehouse.'

'Have you ever seen 'em smoking?'

'Yes, sideways.'

'How many?'

'About 10.'

'Right, 10 Chinese, how many brands of fags are there?'

'About a score*.'

'So, without going to China, you've seen *10* Chinamen smoking; now, out of 20 brands of fags, one brand is Woodbines, therefore on the law of averages at *least* half a per cent of the Chinamen are smoking Woodbines.'

'Whoever saw half a Chinaman smoking?'

'Why don't you bleedin' idiots go to sleep,' said a weary voice. A good idea. The bleedin' idiots went to sleep. Not before a German plane dropped parachute flares, bathing our faces in an eerie green light.

'You're going mouldy,' says Edgington. 'No, I'm not,' I said, 'I'm inventing Penicillin.' Another flare, this time red. Lovely.

'He's trying to make us think it's Guy Fawkes night.'

* 20.

'He's taking photographs,' said Harry.

'Say Cheese.'

The flare faded, the plane droned away, I suppose the pilot was as pissed off with war as we were, in half an hour he'd be in bed smoking a fag and playing with himself, or if rumours about the Germans were true, playing with his fag and smoking himself.

'You still awake Harry?'

'No, I'm dead asleep, this is a recorded message.'

I yawned one of those yawns that makes the back of your head touch your shoulder blades and push your chest out. Tomorrow the new Gun Position. Oh no! *not* tomorrow . . . *at midnight* we were beaten awake with rifle butts, our erections smashed down with shovels. We were to move *now*.

'This isn't war,' screamed Edgington, 'it's Sadism. S-a-d-e-s-e-a-m' etc. The convoy crawled along in pitch darkness, the moon having waned. 'Where are we going sir?' I asked.

'It's a place called Map Ref. 517412,' said Lt Goldsmith.

'They don't write numbers like that any more sir.'

We passed the bombed shattered village of Toukabeur, full of Booby Traps. Seven Sappers were killed during clearing. Outside the village was our new position. At night it looked like the surface of the moon, or Mae West's bum the moment the corsets came off.

In front of us was a rocky multi-surfaced outcrop 80 feet high and a hundred yards long, behind us a ledge dropping sheer 50 feet to a granite plateau 50 yards long, then another 30 foot drop into a valley, in fact two giant steps. The canvas command post erected, I pitched my tent on the edge of the first drop, because shells falling behind me would drop 50 feet down and I would avoid being sub-divided by the Third Reich. However, if shells landed in front of me, I'd suffer the quincequonces. The guns were pulled, heaved and sworn into position. Wireless network opened with 78 Div. H.Q. and 46 Div. O.P. line laid and contact made. Jerry dropped an occasional Chandelier flare. Kerrashboom-kerak! Our first rounds went off at 22.00 hours. I was on Command Post duty all night.

A Sgt standing on the trail to make it more difficult to move

In between fire orders a running argument developed between Lt Beauman Smythe, Gnr Thornton and self.

Thornton: There's been heavy casualties on Bou Diss.

Me: I'm glad it's not me.

B-Smythe: That's a selfish view.

Me: Selfish Sir? All I said was I'm glad it wasn't me that died.

B-Smythe: That's not something to be *glad* about!

Thornton: I think –

Me: Sir! You want me to say 'I'm sorry it wasn't me that got killed'?

B-Smythe: It's better than being *not* sorry. Someone's got to get killed in wars.

Me, Well, someone *was*, it's just that it wasn't me.

Thornton: I think –

B-Smythe: I still say your attitude to death was selfish.

Me: Look sir, mother went thru' a lot of pain to have me, I was a 12 lb. baby, 11 lbs. was my head, me father spent a fortune for a Sergeant on my education, some days it was up to threepence a day, I'm not throwing all that away. My father still goes round with a begging bowl.

Thornton: I think –

B-Smythe: I still say your attitude to death was selfish.

Milligan: Shellfish?

Thornton: I think –

Me: Sell? What *do* you think?

Thornton: . . . Oh Christ – I've forgotten.

Me: Well be a good boy, go outside and get killed to cheer up Lt Smythe.

Off duty at 06.00 hours, went straight to bed and I think I died.

Trauma

'Panzers!' hissed a voice. I could hear the bogies screeching on the iron tracks, suddenly it loomed above me, the track pinioned me and crushed my feet. I felt the bones snap, it was coming up my thighs, I screamed blood, the monster was pushing my stomach up into the chest cavity. I could feel my intestines being forced up my throat, the blood was being squeezed up into my head, my skull burst under the pressure, my eyes were hanging on my chest, I was vomiting my intestines . . .

April 14. Wednesday. 1943. Midday, guns didn't wake me but Lunch did. In daylight our newly painted green and yellow guns stood out dangerously against the chalk white surroundings, but, by ingenious draping with dark and light grey blankets they blended in splendidly. 'It would have been better if we'd painted the bloody rocks yellow and green,' said crazed voices who had to wait all day to get their blankets back and then rise at dawn to give them up again. Our O.P. was in a dodgy position on Djbel Chaouach being under mortar fire, hence the small sign by the O.P. trench. 'For sale – no reasonable offer refused, owner forced to sell, apply Fear and Co.'

At short notice I was rushing up to Chaouach O.P. to collect some dead batteries, idiot driver Cyril Bennett parks wireless truck in full view of Jerry, mortared to hell before we drove to safety.

Drawing – German tank 'Brewing up' Beja–Medjez Road

'Why did they shoot at us,' said Driver Bennett, 'they could *see* we wasn't armed.' Today that driver is Anthony Barber M.P. Another parcel from home! Fruit cake, holy medals, and soapy cigarettes. I divided the cake among the poor of the parish, we ate the lot in 20 minutes, it was a question of getting as much down you as soon as you could before the word got round. Chater Jack had got wind of it and entered the C.P. to find men with cheeks bulging.

'What are you eating?' he said, his voice slightly strained. Lt Beauman-Smythe said 'Wegge eaghting schom of Milligan's Chake Suh,' sending out a stream of air borne crumbs in the Major's face. Chater Jack scanned the cake flecked maw. 'Any left?' he said hopefully but with dignity. I held up the empty tin. Chater Jack paused, clenching and unclenching his fists. 'Next time Milligan . . .' he never concluded the statement, like a Napoleon at Waterloo he turned, and left.

15 April 1943. Hooray! I discovered a hand hewn room in the face of a cliff below our Command Post. Safety at last! I moved in. I awoke at 3 a.m. to the patter of tiny feet, I was crawling alive with fleas. I suppose delousing by the light of a candle could be considered 'non essential war work.'

0600: On duty again, a mass of bites and scratches.

'What in Christ's wrong with your face?' said Gunner Thornton.

'Nothing *wrong* with it,' I said thru' a thousand blotches. 'It's the new Helena Rubenstein Gunners Dawn-Kiss make up, it will soon be the rage of the 1st Army.'

'What's it called?'

'Stage One Leprosy.' Let me describe Thornton, 36, old for a Gunner, but young for an Englishman, 5 foot 11 inches, about 11 stone, the removal of his boots brought him down to 8 stone. A handsomish face in the Gregory Peck mould but obviously there wasn't room in the mould for him. Blue eyes with an honest frank look, even honest Jim, he smoked a briar pipe that only rested when he washed or slept, he never laughed out loud, primarily because his teeth shot out, he had a habit of scratching the back of his left hand whenever he was thinking, that's why he never scratched the back of his left hand. The phone buzzed. 'Command Post Answerin',' I said. It was the O.P. 'Action Stations, Moving Target, Range 11,500! . . . Angle of sight 45°! H.E. 119! Charge 4, Fire!' The guns burst into shuddering iron monsters, just as the dawn in all its majesty was coming up like thunder, but I couldn't have cared a fuck less. I returned to my rocky room with a tin of D.D.T. put in fresh straw. Later that day, I arranged to allow Gnr Shapiro to move in with me during air attacks, at 2 fags a raid.

Through the hot afternoon we lay in our cool stone bower playing battleships. Suddenly an air raid explodes on the area, '2 fags!' I said. Guns were going off in all directions, the sky a mass of explosions, shouts and yells, sounds of men running like the clappers. 'It must be hell out there,' said Shapiro calmly. We looked at each other, the thought of all that shit flying about outside, with everybody crashing into each other was too much, we cried with laughter. I loaded my captured German rifle and loosed off a few rounds at a plane. It was one of ours. 'Never mind,' said Shapiro. 'You tried.' Our safe arbour soon became known, the next air raid there was a thunder of approaching boots, and 20 gunners dived into my tiny hideaway, 'Two fags a time!' I shouted from underneath.

Meanwhile with Tito in Jugoslavia
The scene: A British Military Mission Drinking Club. It is made from packing cases. Inside, beside a hand crank gramophone, two British Officers are drinking 'Buggery-and-Pissed-out-of-your-Mind Champagne'.

RANDOLPH CHURCHILL: When I grow up I'm going to sue everybody for a living.

EVELYN WAUGH: I'm braver than you.

RANDOLPH: No you're not, my daddy's Winston Churchill.

WAUGH: He's a silly poo!

RANDOLPH: Step outside and say that.

Waugh goes outside.

RANDOLPH: That's got rid of him!

WAUGH: (distant) He's not out here!

WAUGH: (returns having just buggered a shepherd) Ah! that's better! I'm braver than you, I wear a woolly outer garment. I'm braver than *anyone*! When a German plane comes over I never take cover, you know why?

RANDOLPH: Yes, you're a cunt.

WAUGH: Don't talk to me like that! When you write your Dad's biography, I want to help you spell Dardanelles!

Enter Tito.

TITO: Haven't you two Herberts cleaned up this Naafi yet?

RANDOLPH: Sorry sir, but we're waiting for SAS to parachute in Brooms.

A bottle of Champagne explodes, all lay on the floor and shout 'I'm braver than you are' while Waugh buggers the lino.

Friday, April 16th. April the 16th. My birthday. I'm 25 years old. I requested the guns to fire a 21 gun salute, they said 'Happy Birthday, piss off.' My family had sent me a birthday card and another 3 holy medals, I now had 103 – I used them as currency with the Arabs.

There was bitter bloody fighting on Djbel Tanngouch, Heidous and Djbel Ang, all of them changing hands several times throughout the terrible day. In support of them, we fired continuously, the Gunners were out on their feet, but knew their lot was easy compared with the P.B.I. so they never complained. There was, however, an occasional cry of 'Fuck this for a livin'.' Lt Tony Goldsmith at the O.P. did some deadly accurate shooting, and remained stoically calm through the most blistering mortaring. In between shoots he would 'phone command post.

'Hello Milligan, I'm going to have a nap, would they turn the volume down on the guns.' He has eight days of his young life left.

Something had held up our rations, rumour hath that
(a) The rail link to the front was bombed.
(b) The rations were bombed.
(c) The Arabs stole it and were bombed.
Whatever, we were put on hard tack for 4 days. It was the first time in the war we had felt peckish. One night Fildes, myself and Hart were told to drive to a deserted farm at Chassart-Teffaha and pick up Lt Tony Goldsmith and Co. We were told, 'Watch out for Jerry Patrols.' It was midnight when we arrived, the white-washed walls of the deserted farm showed blue in the moonlight. The engine stopped, the silence that followed was very eerie; we were in a quiet valley, the sound of guns blocked by the surrounding mountains.

'Christ it's quiet,' said Fildes.

'BANGGG,' I said. 'Is that better?'

'Don't take the piss Milligan or from now on I'll play in F sharp.'

'Steady, Driver Fildes, you are a-speakin' to one of His Majesty's Non-commissioned H'officers of two months' standing and four years layin' down.'

'Christ, it *is* quiet,' says Gnr Birch.

'I'll sing a song then.'

Very softly I commenced 'Oh God our Hope in Ages Past' and ever so gently the lads joined in. We did one chorus.

'Well, that has passed,' I said looking at my watch, 'one minute three seconds of World War II in a most peaceful, harmonious manner.'

'I've got a pain in my balls,' said Driver Bennett.

'So have I,' I said, 'his name is Lt Joe Mostyn.'

'Is it safe to smoke here?' said Gnr Pool.

'No! no matter *where* you smoke it's dangerous, it destroys the lungs and stunts the growth.'

'I've smoked 40 fags a day since I was 16 and I'm 6 foot 2 inches.'

'*But! if* you '*adn't* smoked you'd have been 18 foot 3 inches.'

'That's a lot of balls.'

'True, if you're 18 foot 3 inches you might need a lot of balls.'

'Where *is* Lt Goldsmith, it's nearly half past one.'

'Are you missing him darling,' I said.

We had got out of the truck, it was getting chilly, we got back in the truck; we had a cigarette, then, asphyxiated by the smoke, we all got out of the truck, where it was chilly.

'Two o'clock, where the bloody hell is he?'

'You're in charge Bombardier Milligan, do somethin'.'

'Stand-at-ease!' I said, 'Now, men, I suggest we get out our blankets, and kip down in the farmhouse in homage to our King.'

''Ow did you get a stripe.'

'I put the wrong jacket on.'

We laid out on the stone floor.

'Supposin' Goldsmith turns up.'

'He can lay on the floor as well, there's no class distinction down here,' I said.

'Christ I feel 'ungry.'

'So do I,' I said.

'I'd love a good dinner now.'

'So would I,' I said.

Driver Bennett says 'You know what I'd like now . . . a large steak, wiv chips, big long golden ones, fried tomatoes.'

'Turn it up!'

'Turn it up,' I said.

'. . . wiv onions, crispy fried . . .'

'Wiv onions, crispy fried,' I said.

'Shut up, you'll drive us all bloody mad.'

'No! I want to hear his dinner, carry on.'

'Carry on,' I said.

'Then *beans*, big heap of *beans*.'

'Stop it! Stop that grub talk,' shouts Fildes. 'It's torture.'

'It's torture.' I said.

There was a 30 second pause, pregnant with rumbling stomachs and gastric juices looking for food.

'Eggs, 3 big fresh farm eggs fried in butter . . .'

'Stop it! or I'll thud you up the cobblers.'

The menu stopped, but after 10 minutes a misery laden voice said, 'You sod, I can't get to sleep thinkin' about it.'

'I don't think we should go on kipping here,' said Alf Fildes, 'They'll all be waiting for us to report back.'

'O.K. lads,' I say. 'Alf's right, back on the truck.'

'What a bloody life; this isn't war, it's silly buggers. Right now Churchill will be lying in bed, swiggin' brandy, smoking cigars,' Driver Cyril puts on his boots. ''Ere, my feet 'ave swelled.'

'No, they haven't, cunt, they're *my* boots.'

Things righted, we drove off. It was 3.30-ish. 'Where the bloody hell have you been Bombardier?' says ashen-faced Beauman-Smythe.

'We've been waiting for Lt Goldsmith sir in the prone position.'

'That was 5 hours ago!'

'He didn't show up sir, and I'm sorry I wasn't killed.'

He grinned. 'Er – I'm sorry I shouted at you, it's not getting much sleep makes me niggley, you'd better get some sleep, you have to go on again at 06.00 hours.'

'Oh lovely, in 40 minutes' time.'

The fighting continued, confusion existed as to who, what and where, only those lonely men crouching in holes on the rocky Djbels knew the score. A note in the diary of Driver Alf Fildes says simply 'Slept with trousers on for a change,' showing the careless rapture of the time. The duties were pretty heavy, guns firing almost non-stop in the day and Harassing Fire at night.

Saturday April 17th: I'm 25 and one day old and I smoke soapy cigarettes. Gunner Edgington is out on M2 Truck, laying a line to the O.P. They stop for tea, it was infusing to a nicety when down came a black bird to peck off his nose in the shape of half a dozen M.E.'s all taking it in turns to bomb, and straff. As one man, our brave lads, pop-eyed with fear and nicotine stained shirt tails, are on the truck which goes from nought to sixty miles an hour in three seconds. Edgington, showing the phlegm of his Island race, runs *back* for the tea, he is overtaking the truck when the M.E.'s let him have bullets thru' the seams of his trousers, at which moment Edgington removes tin hat and places it over the tea. Save shrapnel pitted mudguards and flattened tyres they escaped unharmed, questioned later about his heroic action, he replied, 'I didn't want any bits to get in.'

Sunday 18 April. Weather getting very warm, all stripped to the waist. Gunner Woods and Driver Tibbs digging trenches.

Woods: 6 foot 2 inches. How far you down?

Tibbs: 5 foot 3 inches. Three feet.

Woods: 6 foot 2 inches. That's no good you want to go down 8 feet.

Tibbs: 5 foot 3 inches. How the bloody hell am I going to get out?

Woods: 6 foot 2 inches. Dig another hole coming up.

It's a dark night, a heavy dew; the order rings from the Tannoy Speaker. 'Fire.' Daddy Wilson echoes 'Fire!' A colossal roar, gunners lean away to avoid the blast, some with hands over ears, the earth shakes, the momentum of the crew carried them automatically to put another shell in, to discover the great gun was missing. They stood, nit-like, poised for action. 'The bloody thing's gone.'

It had indeed, bouncing backwards, over a cliff and crashing 50 feet below, just missing the tent of a sleeping Gunner Secombe of 321 Bty, 132 Field Regt. Like the Nazarene, the

Sergeant, carrying an oil lamp was given to going among 25 Pounder gunners 'and he sayeth "Blessed are they that have seen 7.2?" "What colour was it?" And he hitteth them.'

Sunday 18th April 1943. Visited by a suspect Irish Catholic Priest. I was sitting in the Command Post drawing naked women on a message pad when he parted the canvas curtain.

'Are dere any Catlicks in here?'

I stood up. 'Yes, father, I am, and so are these nude women I've drawn.'

He was about 5 foot 4 inches, and painfully thin, his little pink neck thrust out the top of his Battle dress jacket like a ventriloquist's dummy, his neck not touching the collar, I don't think his body was in touch with his B.D. either. When he sat down I nearly had hysterics, the neck disappeared down the jacket, the collar coming up under his nose. He had bright blue eyes, which blinked very slowly like an owl, he sat there with a huge grin on his pink face, he looked at me and grinned, he looked at Lt Beauman-Smythe and grinned, finally he looked at Bdr Deans and grinned.

'Would you like a cup of tea, Father?' said Lt Beauman-Smythe.

'Er – no tank you, I had one at the 5th Mediums, and annuder before dat at 155 Field, and annuder with the 6th Anti-Tank, and before dat . . .'

'Would you like a tot of whisky?' interjected Beauman-Smythe.

'Oh, now, dat would be nice,' he said and took his hat off.

'He's going to stay,' I thought. Beauman-Smythe drew from his buttock pocket (it used to be his hip but his braces had stretched), and poured a measure into the silver cup. 'Now dis is nice, dis is verry nice,' said the little priest, he sniffed it, 'Ah, dat smells real nice,' then, my God!!! in a flash he THREW it down his throat. Beauman-Smythe was so stunned all he could say was 'Are you all right Father?' 'Well,' he said, getting to his feet, 'I better be going.' Yes, you better, I thought. We stood up, he left. Beauman-Smythe was thunderstruck, 'Are all Catholic priests like him,' he said. 'No sir, some are much taller,' I said.

Mortars, Light Machine Guns and 88's were making it almost impossible for our O.P.'s to direct fire. To help out, an Air O.P. was allocated to us, an Auster craft containing a Pilot/Gunner Officer (the late Tom Sloan of BBC-TV was one). We started fine and then suddenly our Radio contact went on the blink, the infuriated Pilot flew over our Command Post and shouted through the window 'Your Wireless all balls,' then rattled off a series of fire orders, and that's how it went on, him flying over shouting orders, me belting outside, belting in shouting the orders over the Tannoy, then belting out to shout 'Guns ready,' he would shout 'Fire in twenty seconds from now,' then rush off to observe fall of shot. By midday I was shagged out. He was polite enough to

Front Line – April 19 1943

fly over us and shout 'Thanks, I'm off,' I replied. 'I thought you'd never bloody well go,' he raised his hat in mock acknowledgement. 'He must have had a good education' Edgington remarked later, 'I mean, controlling the plane and issuing fire orders at the same time.'

'Education isn't everything.'

'You're right, for a start it's not elephants.'

19 April 1943. On duty at C.P. from 22.00 hours till 02.00. Awakened at dawn by German planes dive bombing 25 pounders in valley behind us. We all sat and enjoyed it very much.

Up front the fighting raged for the peaks dominating the way to the plains before Tunis. Boston Bombers, 60 at a time, went over and blasted the peaks, so much explosives were rained on Longstop, it changed the contour of the summit.

24 April. Fighting on Long Stop at a crescendo all day. O.P. under murderous fire – support group at bottom of hill also under heavy shell fire. Gunner Collins hit in hand. At about 11.10 I heard the dreadful news, Lt Goldsmith had been killed. Alf Fildes noted in his diary 'Learn with regret we have lost our best officer.'

I went back to my cave and wept. I remember calling his name. After a few minutes I straightened up, but the memory of that day remains vivid. Apparently, he and Bdr Edwards

Two Infantry men take cover from LGM fire

PERSONAL TRIBUTE
LIEUTENANT A. M. GOLDSMITH

Flight Lieutenant Terence Rattigan writes:—

The loss in action of Anthony Goldsmith, at the age of 31, will be most bitterly felt not only by his many personal friends but by all those who, through his writing, recognized his great gifts and were hopeful of the promise they gave. I have known him intimately for most of his life, for we were at Harrow together, and later at Oxford, where Tony was an exhibitioner of Balliol. His quiet, humour, deep intelligence, and gentle, unfailing charm endeared him at length to many whom his shyness and modesty at first repelled. His outlook and views, though never at all forcibly expressed, might have appeared at times to the unthinking acquaintance as too self-consciously heterodox. They were in fact the product of his extreme honesty, his tolerant understanding of human weaknesses, and his exceptionally adult mind. He was witty in the best sense: he combined the happiest knack of phrase with a warmth and a generosity that put malice out of bounds. His remarks were freely quoted, but were never made for that purpose. Indeed, so poor—from the stand-point of the professional wit—was his delivery, so grave and unassuming his manner, that it was often with a shock of surprise that one realized that one had heard—but barely heard—an observation at once breath-takingly honest and brilliantly funny.

The same delicious and distinctive quality pervaded his writing. Very little time was granted him in which to make his mark as an author—barely three years between his decision to devote his life to writing and his joining the Royal Artillery. Much of that time was spent in a painstaking and devoted translation of Flaubert's "L'Education Sentimentale," which many critics found a model of the translator's art. Of original work he has left pitifully little—two plays, one unproduced, a few short stories, and some articles of which a review of the modern theatre in a recent issue of *Horizon* affords an excellent specimen. Little enough to console us—and we were many—who had faith in his right to success and fame. Yet, perhaps those who loved him may take this consolation. Tony, the first to laugh at the futility of the violent passions and the last to covet a hero's laurels, died fighting gladly against that evil which, above all things else, he loathed and despised with a hatred alien to his very gentle nature were sheltering in a fox hole. '*We were under mortar attack, we sat facing each other, our knees touching. Tony had the map board on his chest, his arms folded round it. Suddenly, I was blown out of the trench. I went to get back in and I saw that Tony had been hit by a mortar bomb in the chest, he died instantly . . . .*' All the boys came back very shaken. 'God knows how the Infantry stick that for two weeks at a time . . .' Bdr Dodds was so 'bomb happy' he went to hospital and never came back. For someone as splendid, kind, intelligent and witty as Tony to be killed outraged my sensibilities. His friend, Terence Rattigan, wrote a personal Obituary in *The Times*. I remember his last words to me. He was about to leave for Longstop.

'It won't be long now, I'd say Tunis in 10 days,' he was patting his pockets, 'Blast I'm out of cigarettes.' I gave him 5 of mine, 'Here sir, have 5 of my soap-saturated Passing Clouds, a holy medal in every packet . . .'

He took them, smiled, tapped the driver on the shoulder and said, 'To battle!'

The evening of the 25th April. The Major called us all around his tent, he was well disposed to the world and his fellow men via a distillery at Kirkintoloch in Scotland. In contempt of the Hun he ordered a bonfire to be lit, gathered us around and told us, 'The last battle is nigh, Alexander has offered the Bosch "Unconditional Surrender," or a watery grave, we'll give him Dunkirk without the evacuation facilities. Now let's have a song.' We sang, there was the smell of victory in the air. Next day, we heard that the 8th Argyle and Sutherland Highlanders had taken Longstop at Bayonet point in one incredibly heroic charge, led by Major John Anderson, who was awarded the V.C. Three days of slaughter for the peak had ended.

Almost immediately we got orders for a hurried move to take up new positions somewhere on Longstop. In the rush Edgington hands me a piece of paper. It read:

Stalin's Order of the day,

(a) Two Lagers.
(b) Packet of Crisps.
(c) Stalingrad.

Hitler chalking slogans in Downtown Berlin Gents Toilet after hearing of the fall of Longstop

'This is vital information, comrade Edgington, this must never fall into enemy hands, it must also not fall into enemy feet, teeth, legs or ears, this must be burnt and you must swallow the ashes,' I said, whereupon he snatched the paper, and ate it! 'Delicious,' he said. 'That's called the Readers Digest.' I said. 'Hurry up,' comes a yell, 'we're going.' Burdened down by kit and sacks of souvenirs, we staggered to the Monkey Truck. 'What's been keepin' you,' says Bombardier Trew. 'My mother and a small pension,' I told him, at the same time hitting him with my big pack. 'Oh dearie me,' says Edgington, 'you have laid a non-com. low, with a blow.' Trew reappeared from behind the kit bags.

'Curse, he's still alive,' I said.

'You silly sod I . . .' Before Trew got further Edgington's kit bag hit him amidships and with a yell Trew disappeared again. We jumped on to the truck, and a great wrestling match twixt the three of us ensued, an interesting spectacle it was, as the truck bumped and bounced hurling the kit and the wrestlers in the air. We finally overpowered the reluctant

Trew. 'Say fainites,' I said, as Edgington put undue pressure on his scrotum. 'Fainites,' he screamed. 'If it weren't for the fact you bastards owe me money, I'd arrest you,' said Trew from the depths of the kit bags where we had buried him. 'That's a terrible insult,' I said, 'we must tie him up.' We both dived on the hapless Trew and – using Telephone Cable – bound him hand and foot. Edgington decided to complete the task, a gag would add to the fun, so an unwashed gunner's kerchief was poked into his mouth. 'The least he can catch is Small-Pox,' I said. 'What's goin' on back there,' shouted Driver Bennett. 'We are carrying out essential readjustments to the British Army Punishment system.'

'MmmmmMMMMMMMMmmmMMMUGHHHH' says Bdr Trew.

'Don't mumble man,' shouted Edgington. 'If you want the screens, say so.' It was dark as the guns were pulled into their new positions. German planes were active, lots of parachute flares. Bombardier Deans offered to help dig a dugout if he could share my tent. Oh what it is to be a man of property.

We dug furiously in the dark, throwing ourselves down when the odd German shell landed. It was 04.30 when we got the tent over the top and our kit moved in.

'If there's no jobs after the war, we can be grave diggers, ha, ha, ha, ha,' I said.

'No point in going to sleep now,' said Deans, 'it'll be stand to in a minute.' We were all posted in pairs around the periphery of the gun positions. It was me and Bdr Deans behind a pile of rocks and scrub. I yawned. He yawned. We yawned. He blew his nose – I didn't blow mine. – 'I wonder,' says Deans, 'why we've got 2 nostrils.'

'I should imagine one is a reserve, in case of a malfunction of the other.'

'But a single nostril would look neater.'

'But dangerous; when I was a kid, I got a bead up one nostril, so what's me mum do? Shuts me gob, blows in the clear nostril, and the bead shoots out the other and hits the cat.' There was a silence. 'I wonder what Jerry's up to,' said Deans. 'He must be up to Chapter II, they're slow readers, it's all them big German words like Trockenbeerauslese that

7.2 Camouflaging on Longstop

slows them up.' The odd shell keeps plopping around us, but strangely were nearly all duds. 'They sound as if they come from Cheesmans of Lewisham,' I said. Beauman-Smythe visited us. 'There's the chance of a counter-attack by Jerry, if he does, we'll be in the middle of it, so keep KV.'

'Thank you for cheering us up sir,' says Deans. 'If they do attack sir,' I said, 'do you want me to get killed right away, or shall I fight for a bit first.' He forced a laugh – 'he, he, he, ha, ha, ha!'

Chater Jack had got us in a very forward position for heavy guns, were in front of all the Field and Mediums, and in view of Jerry. Dawn came and went, and our camouflage must have been good because no rangeing rounds came over. We were told not to move about too much and to keep in our particular fold in the hill in which the guns were secreted, some of the lads wandered out into view and were immediately nailed by an 88 Battery. Spiv Convine found a heavy German Machine Gun, which he tried to sell to Lt Mostyn. 'I'll have to have it valued first,' said Mostyn, 'you never know, it might be a fake. I must also arrest you for not handing in an enemy weapon thereby contravening Kings Rules and Regulations.' Convine staggered back and held his head.

'What's wrong man,' said Mostyn.

'I think I've got an attack of Anti-Semitism coming on sir.'

'Good heavens,' said Mostyn, 'I must be a carrier.'

'Has anybody seen Bombardier Trew,' said Sergeant Dawson.

A nasty feeling came over me. Trew was found, purple with fury where we had left him the previous evening, underneath the kit bags. Edgington and I later saw him stalking around with an iron bar in his hand and kept well clear. That morning Lt Beauman-Smythe is reccying our area for a better position (like Bexhill I tell him), when four Germans with hands aloft come out of a dugout. 'Kamerad,' the spokesman says. Smythe, unfamiliar with Saxons, was embarrassed. 'Shoo,' he says, 'clear off.'

'Kamerad Herr General,' they insisted.

'You Nix Prisoner, me busy, clear off,' he said in his best Rugby Referee voice. However the Germans followed him like lost children.

'Oh Christ, get them on the truck, and drive them away.'

'Where to sir,' says Driver Bennett.

'*Anywhere!* Take them somewhere, tell them to get off – say Shoo! – then drive away.' So Bennett drives them into the vicinity of the 5th Medium Regiment, drops them off and leaves them, whereupon the hapless Germans were immediately fired upon by the Gunners.

26 April

Gunner Driver Alf Fildes writes in his diary:

'*Spike kindly sleeps all day, while I use match sticks, 5 hours sleep in 2 days. I think I'll hand my blankets in for the duration.*'

Now for the love of me I don't remember sleeping all day! *My* diary says,

'*Fildes kindly sleeps all day, while I use match sticks, one hour's sleep in eight weeks, I can't go on like this! Worse still last night I caught Alf Fildes copying something from my diary. In the morning I'm going to tell teacher.*'

O.P. reported a five hour tank battle, some using flame throwers. 6th Armoured vs the X Panzers. M.E. 109's bombed vehicles using the Medjez el Bab Tunis Road, but ran into well concealed Beaufort Guns that shot two down in flames amid whoops of jubilation from the lads. Part II Orders: '*The sheik from Medjez-el-Bab has complained to General Anderson that chickens are being stolen by Allied Troops, this practice*

Local Arab reporting 19 Battery to the Sheik

will stop forthwith. Any one seen in possession of a chicken will be questioned, and will have to show proof as to how he came by it.' 'Oh Fuck!' says Chalky White. 'There goes two months' free dinners.'

A swelling had started on my knee. I said so to Lt Budden.

'A swelling has started on my knee.'

'It's got to start somewhere,' he said.

'True,' I said, 'I hope it's nothing trivial.'

I hobbled about dropping hints, 'Oh dear, *there* it goes again, tsu! tsu! . . . I hope it does not get any worse, or dearie me, I will have to stop serving my King and Country and he will have to serve himself!' The knee got worse, I reported to the M.O., a laconic Canadian who looked like Charles Boyer and dribbled. 'Yur, you've got some kind of infection, I think it's a blind boil.'

'Does this mean an optician?'

He wrote something on a bit of paper that looked like 'Asparagus tetani-scrotum.' To a Field Hospital I went, a series of tents on an arid plain near Beja. A man, disguised as a female nurse said 'Undress, lie on that bed, and die!' I pulled on blue military pyjamas that had remained unchanged, and I suspect unwashed, since the Crimea. The tent was a hundred feet long, beds lining the walls, filled with various 'non combatant' ailments, i.e. boils, piles, flat feet, dandruff, varicose veins and cowardice. To my left a Grenadier Guardsman with bunions, to my right a Corporal with Mange. Nurses go around every morning at 4.00 and stick thermometers in your mouth or up the anus. I had mine orally, I prayed every morning I'd get it *before* the first of the rectums. A red-faced pissed sandy-haired doctor stopped at my bed, looked at my chart.

'You're shuffering from Milligan?'

'No sir, that's my name.'

Next day he said, 'Bad knee I shee!'

Next day, 'We must have a look at it.'

Next day 'What's the matter with you?'

'I'm suffering from a recurring amnesiac sandy-haired doctor.'

I was given massive doses of the new drug, Penicillin. The

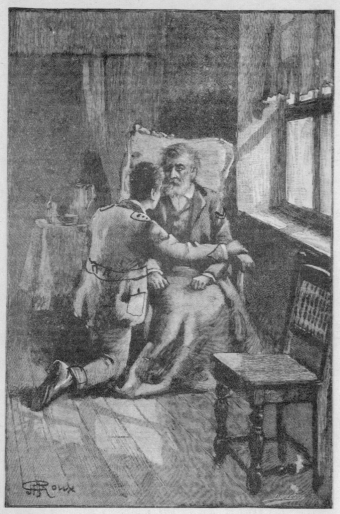

A prematurely aged L/Bdr Milligan being told by the M.O. he must stop screwing Nurse Sheila Frances or go blind

knee subsided, but *I* started to swell, my temperature soared. What luck! I was allergic to Penicillin! I spent three wonderful days in clean bedsheets, and visits from the WVS ladies.

'What are you ill with?'

'Penicillin poisoning, mam.'

'You brave boy. Your parents must be so proud of you.'

'No, they think I'm a silly bugger.'

She smiled. She was deaf. The ground temperature was 100° as she gave me a woollen pullover, scarf and gloves. 'It gets very chilly in the evenings,' she added. A kind old dear, but the wrong kind, I think her name was Trowler, she was about a hundred and sixty, and always carried a shovel. There was one magnificent nurse, Sheila Frances. She had red hair, deep blue eyes and was very pretty, but that didn't matter! because! she had big tits. Everyone was after her, and I didn't think I had a chance, but, she fancied *me*. I got lots of extra, like helping me get her knickers off in her tent and she eased my pain no end. It was all very nice but had to end, one morning I was loaded on to a truck driven back to the regiment for a well-deserved rest. Every night after that I would face in the direction of the hospital, take all my clothes off and howl.

Trauma

I couldn't move. Something terrible was about to happen. Something so awful, that only in dreams would it be concerned, and yet it was about to become a reality, a German 115 mm shell was in orbit, and on a collision course with my body, it was going to explode when it touched my groin, my bowels were going to be blown out of my back, yet I would still be alive long enough to turn and see my entrails traced out fan-like from my stomach, I would hear a high-pitched scream, it was my mother, she was standing in the front room – and I lay on the carpet, outrageously mutilated.

Battery Diary: April 27th

Lt Goldsmith buried on LONGSTOP.

My Diary April 30th

Back from Hospital and recovering from sexual coma. Early duty in Command Post. Duty Officer Lt Beauman-Smythe.

The Battery was heavily engaged in Counter Battery Fire, we silenced German 88s at Montresier and again at Djbel Bou.

'Why must we always drop bleedin' great shells on 'em to shut 'em up.' This is L/Bdr Milligan addressing the Command Post.

'Well what do you suggest?'

'We could write to them, and say "you are causing a disturbance, please keep quiet, otherwise we will drop heavy explosive things on you".'

'Look,' says Signaller Birch, 'the Germans are thick, thick, thick, if you belt a Kraut over the nut with a sledge hammer you have to tell 'im to fall down.'

'Give me a cigarette, and I will agree with you.'

'Gord, you still scrounging fags, how many do you smoke a day?'

'As many as I can cadge, in civvy street I smoked sixty a day.'

'That's too many mate.'

'Yes, it was too many, but some days, it was just right.'

'They'll kill you in time.'

'*Something* kills *everybody* in time, take my grandmother, she died of deafness.'

'Died of *Deafness*?'

'Yes, there was this steamroller coming up behind her and she didn't hear it.'

'She didn't die of deafness . . . she died of steamroller.'

So the dialogue went on between fire orders. Then at midday, we were in the middle of a counter battery shoot against enemy Guns at Djbel Guessa when we heard what I thought was an unusually loud explosion from one of our guns. I failed to get any acknowledgement of fire orders from A Subsection. 'A Sub are you hearing me . . . .'

Something had gone wrong, then a startled voice came through my headphones. 'Command Post, we've been hit,' a gasp and then silence. We all started to run to the guns, which were about thirty yards away screened from us by a small feature in the hill. What we saw was terrible, the entire crew of A Sub section lay dead, dying and wounded around their gun. At first we all thought it was a direct hit by Jerry, but it was an even bitterer pill to swallow. B Sub Gun in the lee of A Sub had fired and their shell had prematurely exploded as it was level with A Sub Gun causing havoc. Lance Bombardier 'Ginger' Roberts lay on his back, blood spurting from his neck. 'Put digital pressure on,' he shouted to a Gunner who was trying to stench the bleeding, but the wound was too huge, he started to lose consciousness. 'I want to write to my wife.' We hurried for paper and pencil. 'The bastards,' he said, 'The terrible bastards.' He still thought it was a German shell, we let him. He started to dictate a letter but lapsed into unconsciousness half way through. Gunner Glanville lay face down, his entire back blown away, he couldn't have felt a thing. Others lay dead, Nicholls, Wood, Glanville . . . the only one unhurt was Smudger Smith but he was staggering about in a state of shock. To stop any decline in morale, the remaining guns were immediately given Gun Fire and soon were blazing away, while, under their muzzles lay the blanket covered figures of the dead. It was bloody awful. I went straight to Beauman-Smythe.

'I've never drunk whisky but if you have any, I'd bloody well like some.' He looked at me 'Of course,' he said, went to his bivvy and came back with a bottle. 'Try that,' he said, handing me a stiff tot and consuming his from the bottle. The ambulance had arrived and the Medics had bandaged up the injured which included Sgt Wilson, Bdr Marston, Bdr Powell, Gunners Convine, McCourt, Wisbey and Howard, and carted them off to the Hospital. What a terrible day.

There was to be a 'Short Arm' Inspection. How Bombardier Morton berated it. 'It shouldn't be allowed' he said, in heavy Welsh tones, starting to undress.

'Why not?' I said, looking forward to the occasion for a laugh.

'What's down there is a man's private affair.'

'They're not going to make it a limited company, it's a medical inspection, that's all.'

'No! that down there is only for the eyes of the woman you love.'

'Only for her eyes? Is she a dwarf?'

7·2 Gun at Longstop firing on enemy Battery

He paced up and down holding his trousers up with one hand, and gesticulating with the other, his face set grim. Occasionally he'd gesticulate with both hands and the trousers fell down. All this because someone was going to have a quick 'butchers' at his Wedding Tackle.

'I don't see any harm in a Doctor lookin' at yer tool' said Gunner Farminer, 'I think a bit of air does it good and let's face it, it's no bleedin' holiday for the Doctor either.' Still grim and grey Morton continued 'You have no pride boyo.'

'No pride?' said Farminer. 'How can you be proud of an 'orrible lookin' thing like that? I mean, if it was beautiful, people would do an oil paintin' of it, but I ain't seen a Portrait of a Prick signed Picasso?' Morton dismissed him with a wave of his hand.

We stood in a queue. 'Drop 'em' was the instruction, a professional eye would scrutinise the honeymoon area, a gesture to turn round – 'Bend Down,' I couldn't resist it, 'Good morning sir' I said through my legs, 'nice day'. 'Not from where I am' said the M.O. There was a round of applause when 'Plunger' Bailey dropped his trousers revealing God's answer to lovely women, even the laconic M.O. was given to nodding his head in approval. A worried Gunner, who we will call 'X', asked to see the M.O. 'privately'. What follows was told me by Medical Orderly Watts. 'X' had been married just before we came overseas, but, his wife had never written him since. He had been harbouring a fear, which he confessed to the doctor 'I think sir, perhaps my private is undersized and my wife will go off with a Polish airman.' The M.O. assured him, 'Lots of men have this phobia but it's all in the mind.' Gunner 'X' insisted. 'Very well, "X" let's have a look.' The surprised M.O. saw that Gunner 'X' had indeed been sold short. 'Yes,' he said, 'Mother Nature hasn't been very kind to you. Does it hurt you?'

'No sir.'

'It doesn't pain or anything?'

'No sir.'

'Can you pass water all right?'

'Yes sir.'

'Well I should use it just for that then.'

Battery Diary

May the 1st. Battery still engaged on Counter Battery Targets. The Offensive launched at end of April has ground to a halt. What now?

I didn't have to wait long for an answer. On the Medjez plain to our right appeared the vehicles of the Eighth Army, all painted sandy yellow, tanks, half tracks, Brens, transports, the lot, the dust they raised was like a sand storm. At night they lit bonfires and the scene looked like Guy Fawkes night on Hampstead Heath. What was happening? Alexander had moved the 4th Indian, the 7th Armoured Div. (The Desert Rats) and 201 Guards Brigade on to our Front, to build up for the final Battle (STRIKE).

The accumulation of Eighth Army Units went on until the 3rd of May. A new officer has arrived to replace Tony Goldsmith, one Lt Walker, dubbed 'Johnny', blonde, blue-eyed, a cavalry moustache, 5 foot 8 inches, quiet, funny – i.e. Laying on a hill in the dark at a dodgy O.P. I heard him draw his Colt Automatic and put a round in the breech. 'What's that for?' I whispered. 'Academic reasons, Milligan' he said. Away from his Bivvy, he left a notice – 'This is a forward office for a Dewar's Whisky Agent, who is authorised to taste

General Montgomery about to start the battle for Tunis

any whisky to verify that it is of the required standard. For this service – there is no charge.'

The arrival of hot weather brought an issue of Khaki Drill. The sight of white knobbly legs plus voluminous shorts brought forth howls of laughter. We looked like ENSA comics trying to look funny.

'What are you writing inside your trousers?' said Edgington.

'It says, "these shorts must never be worn in sight of the Enemy . . .".' The sun never sets on the British Empire – with these shorts it would never set on their knees either.

'Bloody mosquitoes! I thought they'd all been killed by the British Army in India,' said heavily bitten Smudger Smith. Indeed they hadn't. Fortunately we were taking anti-malarial Mepacrin tablets three times a day, with unfortunate results, for some gunners turned yellow. Gunner Woods went to sleep an Anglo Saxon and woke up a Chinaman.

'Oh, look, chop-chop,' I said. 'You fightee Jelly Soldier disgluised as Chinky Poo.' Poor Woods, a simple man, went into a depression. 'It'll wear off,' I consoled. 'It won't, I been

Terrible effect of Mepacrin on Gunner Woods

trying' to wash it orf all morning, I rubbed the skin orf and it's still yeller underneath.'

'What you need' said Lt Joe Mostyn, 'is a solicitor. In your condition you could sue the British Army for altering your nationality without your permission.' Fortunately for the Chinese race the effect of Mepacrin wore off after a week. It was about this time that I saw something that I felt might put years on the war. It was a short Gunner, wearing iron frame spectacles, a steel helmet that obscured the top of his head, and baggy shorts that looked like a Tea Clipper under full sail. He was walking along a gulley behind a group of officers, heaped with their equipment. It was my first sight of Gunner Secombe; what a pity! We were so near to Victory and this had to happen. I hadn't crossed myself in years, and I remember saying, 'Please God . . . put him out of his misery.' I never dreamed, one day he, I, and a lone RAF erk called Sellers, at that moment in Ceylon imagining he could hear tigers, would make a sort of comic history, not that we were

200

Gunner Edgingtons expressive drawing of L/Bdr Milligans 1st appearence in shorts

Gunner Chalky on the 1st Day of K.D issue.

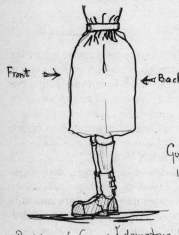

Front ⟹   ⟸ Back

Profile of Gunner Edgingtons legs on 1st day of Shorts K.D

not making it now; oh no – every day was lunatic. What can you say when Gunners taking mobile showers get a sudden call to action? Imagine the result – the sight of a gun team in action, naked, in tin hats and boots, all save Bombardier Morton who holds his tin hat afront of that part which only his 'loved one should see.' As I stood there I thought 'My God, what havoc one determined German could wreak on this lot with a feather duster.'

'You lot, Ammunition *Fatty gues' says Sgt Dawson with all his hate glands going.

'Not me sarge' I said, 'I'm a Catholic – today's Ash Wednesday, a day of obligation.'

'Today's Thursday.'

Have you ever tried off-loading 200-lb. shells for three hours on Ash Thursday? The effect on my back was more devastating than twenty minutes with Louise of Bexhill. At the O.P. Lt Walker and Bombardier Deans were carrying out a pleasurable shoot. Now Germans don't like 200-lb. shells landing on their nice clean tanks, it spoils the paint-work, but there was Lt Walker landing nearer and nearer with every shot until – ker boooom!

'You've hit one' says Deans.

'It wasn't the one I aimed for,' said Lt Walker.

B.S.M. MacArthur, the Bore of Tunisia turns up at the G.P. and spends the night in the gun crew's bivvy. He starts, '. . . among my friends are Lord Beaverbrook, The Lord Mayor of London, Sir Edmund Speers, The Earl of Caer-narvon . . . .'

A voice from a dark corner, 'Don't you know any fucking dustmen?'

'You're on a charge for insolence to an NCO.'

'Shall I wear full court dress, or could you stand me wearin' KDs?'

The tent went quiet save for a few stifled laughs. The offending Gunner got off with a caution, and B.S.M. Mac-Arthur was told by the presiding Major to try and avoid – 'boring the arse off tired soldiers with late night fairy stories,

* Fatigues.

and something else, I *know* Lord Beaverbrook personally and I tell you straight, he's never bloody heard of you.'

The end was near for the quarter of a million Axis troops. Our build up of tanks, troops and artillery was massive, the weather was now really hot, bone dry, and dust was the most prolific element of our daily lives.

May 2nd Battery Diary:

B.C. to O.P. Enemy Battery observed active 62356 engaged by 19 Battery and silenced. Enemy guns active from DJBEL GUESSA, Favourable Meteor brings them within range of 19 Battery, effective observed, fire continued till last light, one enemy troop silenced the others out of range.

Well, that took care of May the 2nd. The third and fourth continued as both sides jockeyed for positions for the final round. 'Bloody 'ell' says an alarmed Gunner Forrest rushing into the Command Post, 'There's bloody black soldiers fightin' on our side.' I explained they were the Fourth Indian Div. 'I didn't know they let 'em fight for us, I thought they was never allowed out of India, I mean can you trust 'em, they're all bloody Wogs. My dad said they were lazy buggers and you couldn't trust 'em.' I explained that nearly a fifth of the Eighth Army was made up of 'Wogs' and all that lay 'twixt him and the Jerry at this moment were in fact Wogs. That night I heard he slept with a loaded rifle by his bed. 'I hope the Germans give 'em a bloody good hiding,' he said. Today that man is Alf Garnett.

We continued various firing tasks, then!

0300 hrs. on the 6th: At that hour, on a very narrow front, 600 guns in two hours dropped 17,000 rounds atop the Baddies. The Infantry moved forward. By 7.30, 6th Armoured started to move forward through a mine-free gap prepared by the 4th British Div., but alas the job had been botched and this slowed up the armour. Overhead there was an unending umbrella of British and American aircraft that bombed and straffed anything that moved, including us. Our battery continued firing at targets chosen by our O.P. The ammunition expenditure was enormous. 'This is costing us a fortune' said Lt Mostyn, 'Honestly, in the last three hours we've spent enough to have opened two hat shops in White-chapel, with a hundred pound float in the till.' I calmed him, 'Would it help if we fired slower, sir?' He shook his head, 'Its too late now, if I had been running this war I could have done it at half the price, I mean what's Churchill know about business? Nothing! Give him a dress shop and in two weeks he'd be skint!'

A gown shop in Whitechapel:

CHURCHILL: Good morning modame.

SHOPPER: I'd like to see a black velvet evening gown with a plunging back.

CHURCHILL: Is that a dress?

SHOPPER: Yes.

CHURCHILL: In two weeks I'll be skint.

A lucky escape by Sergeant 'Maxie' Muhleder whose gun prematurely exploded at the muzzle but no one was hurt. Lt Mostyn rushed to congratulate Muhleder on his escape – at the same time trying to sell him an insurance policy.

In the heat of the final battle, the intense use of artillery never gave much time for anything except moaning.

'If this is bleeding Victory, I prefer stalemates.'

'Even if we win the war, the bloody Germans won't admit defeat, they'll say, "Ve came second".'

Diary May 7th, 2.45 a.m.

On the Command Post wireless I picked up the electrifying message – '6th Armoured and 7th Armoured Units on outskirts of Tunis!'

I threw the headphones in the air. It was round the battery in minutes, everybody was grinning – this was it!

𝕳itlergram 𝕹o. 32b

A bankrupt Gown Shop in Whitechapel that went skint in two weeks.
Scene: The bunker, Hitler is ironing Himmler's head.

HITLER: If we do not vin, zer war ve vill come *second*!

HIMMLER: I have zer Victory Plan. Ve vill burn all zer top Jews.

HITLER: Idiot! London is a smokeless Zone.

HIMMLER: Zen ve vill only burn smokeless Jews.

Terrible clanging sound as Hitler brings coke shovel down on Himmler's head.

Cermans burning their rifles prior to the fall of Tunis

'The Major wants us to look out our white lanyards for the Victory Parade' said Lt Walker. 'Just this once' I said.

'Prepare to move, we've got the bastards holed up in Cap Bon' said Sgt Dawson. The great chase started. We passed swarms of prisoners and gave them the usual treatment.

We raced along the dust choked road to Grich el Oued. Across the great baked plain of the Goubellat we thundered in concert with Infantry and Tanks, all shouting and yelling with the excitement of the kill. 'The Kill!' for that's what it was. Here was I, anti-war, but like the rest of us feeling the exhilaration of the barbarian – it's just under the surface folks, so watch out! B.S.M. MacArthur almost mummified in dust goes down the column. 'It's all over!' he's shouting – and it was! We camped at Oued Melah, told to 'stand alert for a call.' It never came. On May the 12th the fighting ceased. The war in Tunis was over. 'Cup of tea?' said Edgington, 'Ah, cheers,' I said, 'Let's tune in to Radio Algiers.' We did.

Abandoned Guns, Goubellat   May 8/9 '43

End of Volume Two

In Volume Three I will tell of our visit to Tunis and the adventures from there on until the Invasion of Italy. Christ knows when I'll get round to writing it, but stay tuned.

A German Kriegs Marine officer approaching under a flag of truce